# Courageous Church Leadership

## The Columbia Partnership Leadership Series
## from Chalice Press

www.chalicepress.com
www.thecolumbiapartnership.org

# Courageous Church Leadership

## Conversations with
## Effective Practitioners

JOHN P. CHANDLER

CHALICE
PRESS
ST. LOUIS, MISSOURI

Bible quotations, unless otherwise noted, are from the *New Revised Standard Version Bible,* copyright 1989, Division of Christian Education of the National Council of the Churches of Christ in the United States of America. Used by permission. All rights reserved.

Bible quotations marked KJV are from the *King James Version.*

Cover art: Comstock, Inc.
Cover and interior design: Elizabeth Wright

See more TCP resources at
www.chalicepress.com

10  9  8  7  6  5  4  3  2  1               07  08  09  10  11  12

**Library of Congress Cataloging–in–Publication Data**

Chandler, John (John P.)
    Courageous church leadership : conversations with effective practitioners / John P. Chandler.
        p. cm.
    Includes bibliographical references.
    ISBN-13: 978-0-8272-0506-2 (alk. paper)
    ISBN-10: 0-8272-0506-6
    1. Christian leadership. 2. Pastoral theology. 3. Interviews. I. Title.

BV652.1.C488 2006
253–dc22

                                                                2006028829

Printed in the United States of America

# Contents

# Editor's Foreword

## Inspiration and Wisdom for Twenty-First-Century Christian Leaders

You have chosen wisely in deciding to study and learn from a book published in **The Columbia Partnership Leadership Series** with Chalice Press. We publish for

- Congregational leaders who desire to serve with greater faithfulness, effectiveness, and innovation.
- Christian ministers who seek to pursue and sustain excellence in ministry service.
- Members of congregations who desire to reach their full kingdom potential.
- Christian leaders who desire to use a coach approach in their ministry.
- Denominational and parachurch leaders who want to come alongside affiliated congregations in a servant leadership role.
- Consultants and coaches who desire to increase their learning concerning the congregations and Christian leaders they serve.

**The Columbia Partnership Leadership Series** is an inspiration- and wisdom-sharing vehicle of The Columbia Partnership, a community of Christian leaders who are seeking to transform the capacity of the North American Protestant church to pursue and sustain vital Christ-centered ministry. You can connect with us at www.TheColumbiaPartnership.org.

Primarily serving congregations, denominations, educational institutions, leadership development programs, and parachurch organizations, the Partnership also seeks to connect with individuals, businesses, and other organizations seeking a Christ-centered spiritual focus.

We welcome your comments on these books, and we welcome your suggestions for new subject areas and authors we ought to consider.

George W. Bullard Jr., Senior Editor
GBullard@TheColumbiaPartnership.org

The Columbia Partnership,
905 Hwy 321 NW, Suite 331, Hickory, NC 28601
Voice: 866.966.4TCP, www.TheColumbiaPartnership.org

# Acknowledgments

Thanks, first of all, to Jesus Christ, the pioneer and perfecter of courage, for his work to welcome and lead me into the Kingdom, on earth as it is in heaven.

Thanks next to Virginia Baptists, historic and current practitioners of courageous church ministry. It is a delight to live among and learn from these practitioners. Special thanks to my visionary leader, John Upton, and to wise and funny mentors Keith Smith and Bob Dale for their imprint on my soul. Nor could I neglect to mention my teammates on the Courageous Churches team ("play hard, play together, play smart").

Thanks then to those from whom I have learned—not only the practitioners interviewed here, who graciously allowed wide access to intimate conversations, but also the scores of leaders, thinkers, teachers, and practitioners who keep changing my mind and heart. Of note here are Sam Hill, Tom Long, Dallas Willard, June Clifford, and Lyle Schaller.

Finally, I wake up every morning in the middle of beauty, truth, and goodness— a courageous community of faith, hope, and love. For this, thanks to my true love, Mary, and to the apples of my eye, Preston and Roland.

# Preface

## Why Courage?

I believe that an accurate way to describe a North American church operating at or near its Kingdom potential today is to say that it is a "courageous church." *Courage* is an emerging moniker for Kingdom congregations in our nation.

In the 1970s, such Kingdom churches often studied *church growth*. Missiologists Donald McGavran, Peter Wagner, Carl George, and others out of Fuller Theological Seminary taught church growth as the application of the social sciences to congregational life. By 1980, seeker-targeting churches, like Chicago's Willow Creek Community Church, were reaching many heretofore unchurched or underchurched people by applying lessons of sociology and psychology pertaining to how people gather, converse, connect, and make decisions.

By the 1990s, church growth was mainstream in many North American congregations. More churches were paying attention to small and large group dynamics, the psychology of what it meant for newcomers to enter new experiences, and how to create "brand" in community consciousness. As a result, many of these churches began to grow, attracting first-time churchgoers as well as returning prodigal dropouts. In growing congregations, a wide spectrum of spiritual experience and maturity often arose among members and attenders. As a result, multiple agendas emerged for the congregation. Churches grew and sometimes discovered that they had imported "growths" for which they had not bargained!

Into this situation came advocates for church *health*. Rick Warren's *The Purpose-Driven Church*[1] and Christian Schwartz's *Natural Church Development*[2] brought to light that not all growth is good growth; cancer, for instance, can be fast-growing. Instead, Schwartz, Warren, and others tried to help churches focus on their central biblical purposes or characteristics. Yes, churches want to reach unchurched people. But what does a congregation hope will happen once attracting these people? Church health teachers have suggested that it is not enough for churches to attract new seekers. Churches must bring people into fuller discipleship once they are there, and must keep the church on task rather than pandering to the lowest common denominators of what will attract newcomers. Warren famously diagrammed concentric circles aiming to help people move into progressive rings of discipleship: from community to crowd to congregation to committed to core.[3]

- *Community:* Those living around your church who never, or only occasionally, attend
- *Crowd:* Those who attend your church regularly but are not members

---

[1]Rick Warren, *The Purpose-Driven Church: Growth Without Compromising Your Message and Mission* (Grand Rapids: Zondervan, 1995).

[2]Christian Schwartz, *Natural Church Development: A Guide to Eight Essential Qualities of Healthy Churches* (Saint Charles, Ill.: Churchsmart Resources, 1996).

[3]For more information about Rick Warren's ministry, visit www.purpose.driven.com.

- *Congregation:* Those who are committed to both Christ and membership in your church family
- *Committed:* Those members who are serious about growing to spiritual maturity
- *Core:* Those members who actively serve in ministry and mission in your church

By the turn of the millennium, though, some felt that decades of focusing on "bringing people in" (church growth) and "aligning the church with its biblical purposes" (church health) was creating internally focused congregations–perhaps to the detriment of the work of the Kingdom in our culture. Certainly there has been an explosion in the number of very large churches in North America in the last three decades, as more congregations applied the lessons of church growth and church health. But there was also gnawing concern that some churches were worlds unto themselves rather than agencies of transformation within their communities.

Conversations among groups like Leadership Network, Off The Map, and Emergent began to gather congregational leaders in learning communities to discuss the shape of "externally focused churches."

In the foreword to Erwin McManus's book *An Unstoppable Force: Daring to Become the Church God Had in Mind,*[4] Brad Smith notes:

> In talking with hundreds of church leaders each year, I've seen two movements of God that seem to cross all boundaries of denominations, geography, and church styles...First, we see church leaders progressing beyond the church growth movement of the 1980s, which opened up a new awareness of the culture around us. They're also moving beyond the church health movement of the 1990s, which created a new emphasis on intentional discipleship. What church leaders are increasingly talking about is church dispersion. We've worked so hard to get people inside the church and on a path to maturity; how do we now move them back outside of the church to serve in the marketplace, the community, and the world? Church growth and church health really don't make sense without church dispersion; yet that may prove to be the most difficult task yet. We like comfort. We like safety. It is a daunting task to change church from a place that serves consumers to a place that creates servants.[5]

The dispersed courageous church views church growth and church health as means rather than as ends. The goal is not to get people into church. The goal is not to get the church "correct." The goal is for the Kingdom of God to advance, "on earth as it is in heaven." Growth and health are necessary but not sufficient for the final work of the congregation. Gathering people into congregations is but a prerequisite to forming them as disciples, which is but a prerequisite to scattering them as influencers in their families, relationships, communities, and the world. The final Kingdom work of the church is transformation of the cultures it is called to reach. The church, like salt and light, impacts the culture of which it is a part, changing it decisively. Not content to withdraw from the world and get its own act

---

[4]Erwin McManus, *An Unstoppable Force: Daring to Become the Church God Had in Mind* (Loveland, Colo.: Group, 2001).

[5]Brad Smith, as quoted in ibid., 8.

together, the dispersed church moves ever outward into "Jerusalem, in all Judea and Samaria, and to the ends of the earth" (Acts 1:8). The courageous congregation joins hands in a circle, yes. However, in that circle people face not each other, but look out toward the world.

As they move out, they leave a mark–the marks of the presence of Jesus. These churches are in their communities as Jesus himself walked and worked in communities. Because these churches proclaim and embody the Kingdom of God, things in that culture are transformed to mirror more fully life in the Kingdom of heaven. As the Lord's prayer says to Our Father in heaven, "Let your name be made holy on earth as it is already treated as hallowed in heaven. Let your Kingdom come on earth as it has already come fully in heaven. Let your will be done on earth as it is already being done in heaven" (paraphrase of Mt. 6:9–10).

I think the way to describe congregations living this prayer in their communities is to say that they are *courageous* churches. But what does it mean to say that a church is courageous? What is courage?

### What Is Courage?

Paul Tillich's *The Courage to Be*[6] explores the history of the concept of courage. Plato's *Republic* viewed courage as the element of the soul located between the intellectual and sensual element of a human being: "It is the unreflective striving toward what is noble. As such it has a central position in the structure of the soul, it bridges the cleavage between reason and desire."[7] This is a view of courage as a "middle" dimension between the reasonable and the sensual.

For Aristotle, the virtue of courage was connected to concepts of nobility, beauty, and sacrifice:

It includes the possible, and, in some cases, the unavoidable sacrifice of elements which also belong to one's being but which, if not sacrificed, would prevent us from reaching our actual fulfillment. This sacrifice may include pleasure, happiness, even one's own existence. In any case it is praiseworthy, because in the act of courage the most essential part of our being prevails against the less essential. It is the beauty and goodness of courage that the good and the beautiful are actualized in it. Therefore it is noble.[8]

The Greek understanding of courage involved moving by degree toward purer human essence. While this could take place on natural, personal, and social levels, over time courage came to be thought of less in terms of beauty and more in terms of nobility and sacrifice. It began to be attached to the notion of bravery, which is most often called for in situations of peril.

Since the greatest test of courage is the readiness to make the greatest sacrifice, the sacrifice of one's life, and since the soldier is required by his profession to be always ready for this sacrifice, the soldier's courage was and somehow remained the outstanding example of courage. The Greek

---

[6]Paul Tillich, *The Courage to Be* (New Haven, Conn.: Yale University Press, 1952).
[7]Plato's *Republic,* as quoted in ibid., 3.
[8]Aristotle, as quoted in ibid., 4–5.

word for courage, *andreia* (manliness) and the Latin word *fortitudo* (strength) indicate the military connotation of courage.[9]

Thomas Aquinas spoke of courage as a doctrine: "Courage is strength of mind, capable of conquering whatever threatens the attainment of the highest good."[10] Eventually theologians identified courage (along with temperance, justice, and wisdom) as one of the four cardinal virtues. These virtues, when grouped with Paul's "faith, hope and love" (1 Cor. 13:13), become the seven saving virtues, which serve as antidote to the seven deadly sins (pride, anger, greed, lust, sloth, gluttony, and envy). Medieval preachers had a field day pairing each virtue as remedy for each vice; most compelling are descriptions of courage as the medicine for sloth. Courage overcomes sloth (Greek *akadeia,* English "acedia," suggesting listlessness and failure to act; literally "I don't care"). A person is courageous when he or she cares enough to move into action.

For Tillich, the pinnacle of Christian reflection about courage arrives in the work of Luther:

> Every work of Luther, especially in his earlier years, is filled with such courage. Again and again he uses the word *trotz,* "in spite of." In spite of all the negativities which he had experienced, in spite of the anxiety which dominated that period, he derived the power of self-affirmation from his unshakable confidence in God and from the personal encounter with him. According to the expressions of anxiety in his period, the negativity his courage had to conquer was symbolized in the figures of death and the devil. It has rightly been said that Albrecht Durer's engraving, "Knight, Death, and the Devil," is a classic expression of the spirit of the Lutheran Reformation and—it might be added—of Luther's courage of confidence, of his form of the courage to be. A knight in full armor is riding through a valley, accompanied by the figure of death on one side, the devil on the other. Fearlessly, concentrated, confident, he looks ahead. He is alone but not lonely. In his solitude he participates in the power which gives him the courage to affirm himself in spite of the presence of the negativities of existence...For the courage of confidence is not rooted in confidence about oneself. The Reformation pronounces the opposite: one can become confident about one's existence only after ceasing to base one's confidence on oneself.[11]

Thus in classical, medieval, and modern thinking, courage as a dimension of human being and human action has been thought of as

> the *beautiful*—a striving toward what is purer, better, and more humane
> the *noble*—sacrificial action putting aside what is comfortable for what is right
> the *virtuous*—the will to care and act in order to overcome structures of sin and evil that threaten what is good

We can hear echoes of these lines of thinking in modern Germanic and Romance language renderings of courage. As Tillich notes, there are two German

---

[9]Ibid., 5.
[10]Thomas Aquinas, as quoted in ibid., 7.
[11]Ibid., 161, 163.

words for "courageous": *tapfer* (connoting "firm, weighty, important") and *mutig* (pointing to the human center, matters of the heart, something like the English "mood").[12] Of course, our English word courage is derived most directly from the French *couer,* meaning "heart."

### Biblical Courage

In the history of Christian thought, courage takes its fullest form when paired with biblical language and imagery. Sometimes courage is united with (and even thought of as identical to) faith, hope, and love. Sometimes the ethical dimension of courage rises to the forefront: the will to act in the face of sloth:

> Courage listens to reason and carries out the intentions of the mind. It is the strength of the soul to win victory in ultimate danger, like those martyrs of the Old Testament who are enumerated in Hebrews 11. Courage gives consolation, patience, and experience and becomes indistinguishable from faith and hope.[13]

Ultimately, the pioneer and perfecter of courage is Jesus himself. Beyond viewing the incarnation as an ultimate act of divine courage, Jesus' life embodies and articulates courage. Consider, for instance, Jesus' modeling in the following:

- *Temptation*–the courage to resist becoming something other than he was called to be
- *Transfiguration*–the courage to refuse to remain on the mountain and simply align with tradition, instead choosing to go into the valley and undertake a new and risky ministry
- *"Take no purse, bag, or sword"*–the courage to resist the siren call of security;
- *Cleansing the temple*–the courage to confront unacceptable commercial and religious practices
- *Gethsemane*–the courage to wrestle with fidelity in the face of danger to yourself and misunderstanding and apathy from your friends
- *Pilate*–the courage to withstand unjust trial with appropriate silence, grace, or correction
- *Crucifixion*–the courage to care for others (his mother, the world), to offer forgiveness in the face of persecution, and to rely on faith in the fire
- *Resurrection*–the courage to say "No!" to the powers of sin and death
- *Emmaus*–the courage to risk a journey with companions when you are not understood; to wait until the time is right to reveal truth; to rebuke, teach, and bless in community
- *Ascension*–the courage to disappear so that others can move forward to lead in the work

Jesus does not define courage so much as he incarnates and embodies it. His courage is ever risking, ever moving out, always seeking full expression of his unique calling from God. In this way, he signals to followers that courage is the will to act in one's own situation with heart, mind, soul, and strength, in all the ways that he himself would act.

---

[12]Ibid., 6.
[13]Ibid., 8.

Thus back to the original question: Why *courage*? Because when Jesus' followers are *dis*-couraged, they need to be *en*-couraged, so that they may be better equipped to act with faith, hope, and love.

## Why *Conversations?*

For all of Plato's dialogues about courage, the most memorable image of courage in classical civilization is Socrates nobly facing a cup of poison. For all of the Bible's conceptual language of courage ("faith, hope, and love"), the most compelling descriptions of it are in the stories that embody it: Moses before Pharaoh (Ex. 6–14), David before Goliath (1 Sam. 17), Peter and Paul before authorities (Acts 4:1–21; 5:17–42; 21:27–26:32), Jesus before the shadow of a cross (Mt. 27 and parallel texts).

Courage is better described than defined. It is more fully perceived inductively, through narrative, than deductively, through principle. There are no "twenty-one irrefutable laws of courage." There are, however, countless portraits of courage in Scripture, and innumerable continuations of those biblical types of courage to be found in congregations today. That is why the heart of this book is in the dialogues with courageous leaders. They are brush strokes attempting to paint some of today's portraits in courageous leadership.

Conversation is an open medium. By definition, it is only a part of something larger than itself. If the conversations I have captured fail to engender further conversations about the topic, then my experiment has failed. A wise reader will not assume that the conversations I have chosen are the only (or even best) conversations needed. Those best conversations are yet to come: the ones that you will have as you identify and then dialogue with other courageous practitioners. I only hope to model the way, to be catalytic for your own future dialogue.

Finally, I am partial to conversations as vehicles for insight because I often learn better "on the sly" than "straight up." Unpredictable living dialogue sometimes produces a rigorous honesty not always found in distilled, static lists. As my friend Bob Dale teaches well,[14] churches are not mechanisms to be engineered, but living organisms—and one must lead living things differently than inert things. It is often said that the church is not an organization but an organism. In that case, organic leaders will become fluent in leadership conversations.

When I plan a motorcycle trip, I sometimes use my American Automobile Association membership to receive a Trip-tik™ (a map with the best routes marked and including suggested points of interest) and design a trip based on sights I should not miss. In this book, I use this same A.A.A. metaphor to point out "must-see" highlights in the leadership conversations. At the end of each conversation, I will offer suggested further questions in hopes of spurring additional conversations.

## Why *Effective?*

I can go no further without offering a significant disclaimer. It may be that, from the vantage point of the Kingdom of God, from a world perspective, and from the sweep of history, the conversations that follow completely trivialize the notion of the courage in the Christian church. After all, for millennia, Christians

---

[14]Robert D. Dale, *Seeds for the Future: Growing Organic Leaders for Living Churches* (St. Louis: Lake Hickory Resources, 2005).

have faced persecution, discrimination, torture, and martyrdom. This is still true in many parts of the world. When North American Christians describe courage as facing up to critique and disapproval from other church members, it may seem incomprehensibly trivial to Sudanese Christians whose definition of courage may be to refuse to bow to Allah and thus suffer the rape and murder of family members. To my worldwide Christian brothers and sisters facing things I can only imagine, I offer salute, solidarity, and, if needed, apology. We need to hear your conversations of courage as well.

Having said that, what is the right adjective to describe and gather the ministry of courageous practitioners who lead North American churches? "Successful" has some biblical precedent, as the good work of Joseph, Joshua, David, and Nehemiah is described this way (Gen. 39:2; Josh. 1:7; 1 Sam. 18:5; Neh. 2:20). But I fear that the word *success* has been tainted and co-opted by a consumer-driven and money-crazy culture in the United States. Is not "successful ministry" more than well-funded ministry?

Perhaps a better alternative is to think in terms of "effective" ministry. Here, there is also connection to a biblical thread:

"… for a wide door for *effective* work has opened to me, and there are many adversaries." (1 Cor. 16:9)

"I pray that the sharing of your faith may become *effective* when you perceive all the good that we may do for Christ." (Philem. 6)

"Therefore confess your sins to one another, and pray for one another, so that you may be healed. The prayer of the righteous is powerful and *effective*. (Jas. 5:16)

If courage is connected with church dispersion and community impact, then it may be wise to think in terms of the "effect" of a leader on a congregation, and, ultimately, the effect of a congregation on a community, culture, or the world.

*Effective* is also a rangy word. The leaders with whom I here share conversation were, at the time of our talk, serving congregations in the United States that measured from the mid-sized to the enormous. They were all led by men who were at least forty years old. However, that obviously does not mean "effective" is solely defined by or limited to churches of a certain size led by men of a certain age. I could mention several women who also lead effective churches throughout the United States. These whom I highlight have been and are effective church leaders because they have had a profound and positive effect on their congregations, which in turn have had profound and positive effects on their wider worlds.

### Why *Practitioners?*

Mary, my wife, is a nurse practitioner in partnership with Michael Devine, a surgeon who specializes in treatment from the elbow to the fingertip. Mary and Mike have very different, but complementary, roles within the practice of Charlottesville Hand Surgery. To oversimplify somewhat, Mike's job is to assess and treat bones, tendons, and ligaments on the operating table. Mary's role is to converse with the patients—often about things not pertaining directly to the hand. "What medicines are you taking? How are things at home? What kind of work do you do?" She often assesses whether patients can read, whether they are likely to be compliant with rehabilitation and medication, and whether they abuse alcohol or drugs. Mary and Mike have learned many times over that the information she gleans significantly impacts the outcomes of patient care and healing.

In that vein, the aim of this book is to help practitioners listen to and learn from other practitioners. It is not an academic or theoretical treatise. It's style is informal, conversational, even colloquial. It is a companion piece to be used in partnership with thoughtful conceptual work on leadership and congregational life.

Well-matched partnerships between theorists and practitioners are wise. Blessed are the architect and general contractor who listen to one another. Happy is the new mechanic who learns both from the repair manual and from the grizzled pro who cannot read but who can fix cars. Savory is the dish prepared not only according to the recipe but also with seasoning "beyond the book" taught from a grandmother's hand. Gifted is the musician who can read the notes but also play beyond them. Smart is the quarterback who learns not only from the sideline and press box, but also from others on the field, especially from other quarterbacks.

This book is by practitioners, for practitioners. I stand at the front of the line to learn from the fine work of church consultants and theorists such as Charles Arn, George Bullard, Bob Dale, Bill Easum, Carl George, and–the dean of them all– Lyle Schaller. But, to continue with sports analogies, this one from basketball, what we learn from fellow point guards in Nikes is different from what we learn from sideline coaches in Guccis. Both kinds of coaching can be valuable; this book aims to provide practitioner coaching–*and* to model how one can solicit ongoing and deeper conversations with practitioners.

Peter Drucker supposedly remarked that the three most difficult jobs in North America are university president, hospital administrator, and pastor of a local church. Congregational leadership is incredibly demanding. It is often discouraging. Sometimes "shop talk" with people who have figured out things that I need to know helps me to get up and at the task again. I hope these conversations will begin to do the same for you.

# Introduction

What makes these leaders noteworthy guides for courageous church leadership? All lead churches that are widely acclaimed for their growth, health, creativity, impact, influence, and courage. All are acknowledged team-builders, yet they bring courageous individual skills to the complex task of congregational leadership. As these diverse practitioners share conversationally, we can receive practical wisdom that will propel us to lead effectively in our own congregational context.

This book contains twelve chapters:

**Chapter 1:** *What We Need to Learn from These Leaders.* What prevents churches from transformational ministry? What are the key leadership issues in the vast majority of North American churches, and how can these issues of leadership be addressed through overhearing conversations with effective practitioners?

**Chapter 2:** *Courageous Span: Bob Russell.* In more than thirty years as pastor of Southeast Christian Church in Louisville, Kentucky, Bob led a congregation to grow from one hundred thirty to over eighteen thousand in average weekly worship attendance. In this conversation a few years before his retirement, he discusses how he stumbled into new levels of leadership in growing one of the largest churches in the country.

**Chapter 3:** *Courageous Conversing: Fred Craddock.* An accidental pastor and legendary teacher of preaching, Fred learned together with a growing, strong congregation. This conversation provides opportunity to reflect on how leaders get "in" and "out" of leadership roles. It also paints a picture of leadership as relational or conversational.

**Chapter 4:** *Courageous Repositioning: David Chadwick.* Blessed with a winsome personality, David helped a dying Presbyterian congregation forge new coalitions. When the church got "stuck" at one thousand in attendance, this pastor courageously helped Forest Hill Church reposition from an organizing center around his personality to one based on values of evangelizing unchurched people. This interview discusses how pastor and people got through the difficulties of this repositioning and tripled in size since that time.

**Chapter 5:** *Courageous Intelligence: Brian McLaren.* A former University of Maryland English professor, Brian helped to launch a new church for graduate students who seemed unable to find a place in established, traditional churches. When the new church seemed to stall, Brian led a "reboot": the community shut down and reevaluated its philosophy of ministry, opening a year later with a new name, location, and purpose. Cedar Ridge Community Church today offers an intelligent evangelistic ministry to highly educated and philosophically sophisticated seekers.

**Chapter 6:** *Courageous Awakening: Michael Slaughter.* Located by a small-town Ohio cornfield, Ginghamsburg Methodist was a declining, mainline, "family chapel" denominational church. Young pastor Mike stirred the small congregation with a Kingdom-sized vision and survived the early battles. The awakening resulted in one of America's most innovative churches, reaching four thousand people weekly in a town of six thousand with multicultural, multisensory, and multimedia ministry.

**Chapter 7:** *Courageous Blending: Leith Anderson.* Three decades of pastoral leadership from Leith have resulted in such a healthy leadership culture that staff members have been known to request the right to attend staff meetings even when scheduled for vacation. The church currently features six worship services with a wide variety of styles, ranging from liturgical to traditional to contemporary. Here, Leith discusses how very different congregations within Wooddale Church blend into a cohesive mission team.

**Chapter 8:** *Courageous Alliances: Lance Watson.* Lance came into a tradition-laden church, neighborhood, city, and state and helped transform The Saint Paul's Baptist Church from a congregation of two hundred fifty members in a downtown neighborhood, to a citywide ministry reaching more than seven thousand in Richmond every week. This conversation reveals how Lance received and communicated the vision to transform a local "7-11" congregation into a regional "mall" church.

**Chapter 9:** *Courageous Diversity: Erwin McManus.* Erwin is, at heart, a philosopher-pastor. At Mosaic, he equips incredibly diverse groups of Los Angelinos to reach a polytheistic city with the gospel of Christ. Confounding customary wisdom about the "homogenous unit principle," this church has demonstrated the ability to reach and include a wide spectrum of people groups. Says Erwin: "I would rather reach one hardcore pagan in Los Angeles than get ten thousand Christians in Atlanta to go to church."

**Chapter 10:** *Courageous Teamwork: Fellowship Bible Church of Northwest Arkansas.* How does a church grow without a senior pastor? Who's "in charge"? One of a growing cluster of "Fellowship Bible" churches, this church has moved beyond a "guru" or "superstar" model of church leadership and into a multifaceted pastoral team demonstrating shared servant leadership.

**Chapter 11:** *Courageous Vision: Steve Chang.* Language congregations often fly unnoticed beneath the radar of Anglo churches. Yet for its sustainable growth, worldwide vision, and disciple-making rigor, The Light Global Mission Church deserves close attention. Steve has led this congregation toward a vision of a campus that is home not only for Korean and English-speaking audiences, but for people of many languages in this Washington, D.C., rim community.

**Chapter 12:** *What We Are Learning from These Leaders (So Far!)* How do insights from this diverse body of courageous leaders inform our hopes of transformational ministry? What are some of the broad-based "take-aways" that will inform our leadership practices? How do their struggles and triumphs inform our stories? As we reflect theologically on the wisdom shared by these practitioners, what can we elucidate and apply to our own leadership contexts? How can we continue to learn from our own leadership conversations with effective practitioners? We close with practical advice on how to find, interview, and learn from the effective and courageous leaders who are all around us.

I hope and pray you enjoy reading this book, at the same time that you distill learnings from the dialogues with these courageous pastoral leaders.

# 1

# What We Need to Learn from These Leaders

*What prevents churches from transformational ministry? What are the key leadership issues in the vast majority of North American churches, and how can these issues of leadership be addressed through overhearing conversations with effective practitioners?*

Research in 2002 from the North American Mission Board showed that the typical Southern Baptist congregation averages about eighty in attendance. "Southern Baptist congregations, like congregations of most religious groups (in North America), tend to be small. Nearly two-thirds of Southern Baptist congregations have 100 or fewer in worship on Sunday morning."[1] This ratio is certainly true in regards to the 1430 Virginia Baptist congregations in my field of service.

Some of the small Virginia Baptist congregations are small out of preference and choice. They find that authentic Christian community is best experienced and expressed in congregations in which every person can call every other person by name. They may wish for occasional or incremental growth, but most are happy with their size.

Other Virginia Baptist congregations, however, experience persistent discontent with the scope of their congregation's ministry. Sometimes this is driven by fears of ongoing viability; the need to grow is fueled by hopes of funding budgets, and of maintaining or creating facilities.

---

[1]Statistics from the Southern Baptist Convention's North American Mission Board (www.namb.net/research).

Many of the restless, though, wish to grow because they are not convinced that their congregation is fulfilling its Kingdom potential. The ache of secular, pagan, agnostic, or spiritually hostile family members, neighbors, and communities impels them toward a hope for a growing gospel impact. Evangelistic fervor and a desire to see their congregations transform the communities they were called to reach keeps many Virginia Baptist leaders awake on many nights. It is not hard for me to imagine that the same is true in tribes outside of my own. And, I might add, this restlessness is not limited to small congregations and their leaders.

In hundreds of conversations with these leaders, I have been amazed at the recurring "pinch points" constricting leaders and churches who feel called toward expanding their congregations' impact in their communities. Over and over, the conversations cluster around three centers, which I name *vision, leadership,* and *structure.* As we look at each in turn, we may put our finger on what we hope to learn in subsequent conversations with effective practitioners.

## Vision

It is often weak or fuzzy vision that prevents congregations from fulfilling their Kingdom potential. On rare occasions, the issue in churches I encounter is that there is little or no vision for the life and mission of the church. More often, our conversations unearth multiple and often competing visions for the church. Leaders sometimes complain about the lack of investment by members in the congregation. That is true for many attenders and nominal members. But my observation is that the more intractable obstacle is that other members are invested in a multiplicity of agendas for the church. These agendas pull in so many directions that forward movement becomes difficult, sporadic, painful, or impossible.

For a church to be courageous, it must be clear and honest about who God is calling it to reach. There are thousands of congregations in North America, and no single one will transform the entire continent. Gallup, Barna, and North American Mission Board research indicates that as many as ten North American congregations close their doors for the final time each day. If your church is not one of those that has closed, then why is it alive? If your church is one of many congregations in a given area, then, theologically, why does it continue to exist?

I posit that if a congregation has not closed its doors, it is alive at the calling and pleasure of God, who wills it to impact *someone.* Your church is God's best hope for reaching some person or people with the good news of the gospel. The founding of a congregation is God's dream for reaching a certain part of the world with the news about the Kingdom Jesus announced. In the book of Ruth, Mordecai urged Esther to fulfill her courageous mission in a dicey situation. "Who knows? Perhaps you have come to royal dignity for just such a time as this" (Esth. 4:14). God allows each living congregation to live "for such a time as this."

Vision is the ability to understand and communicate the calling of God for a congregation. What we need to learn about vision in our conversations with effective practitioners can be summarized as follows:

*Clarity among the clutter of messages.* Most leaders are conflicted internally and driven by different things at different times. Perhaps one direction for vision is generated by a crisis in the soul or in the congregation. Perhaps another glimpse of vision comes from being moved by the impact of another local or national ministry. What would a spiritual discernment of God's vision for a congregation look like? If we can glimpse impressionistically how others came to internal clarity about vision in leadership, perhaps this would offer pathways for us to do the same.

The other issue of clarity among a clutter of messages pertains to how leaders deal with all-too-clear but competing visions for the church. If God speaks not only to the pastor but to other leaders in a congregation, how are those divine messages formed into a coherent, clear calling for the church? And, when there are irreconcilable differences in expressed vision, how does a leader remain humble, dogged, and clear? How is vision formed in community?

In an age of information and message overload, how do leaders identify, name, and vocalize the core calling of the church?

*Courageous honesty.* In a personal conversation with Lyle Schaller, I asked about what competencies would be required of congregational leaders in coming years. Schaller created a short list:

> Listening skills are number one. Number two is patience…The final thing leaders will need is courage. At least one piece of courage is the willingness to tell the truth. To say what is not politely or politically acceptable. To be the one required to run counter to the thrust of what's going on. Now, I put listening and patience ahead of courage, because if you speak too soon, you'll simply be viewed as disruptive, and your comments get brushed off. You have to be patient to wait to say the courageous word, the courage to tell the truth.[2]

As I began to probe what this truth-telling courage might look like, Schaller recounted his personal experience as a parish consultant. What he as a consultant was charged with saying, many leaders within congregations must, in courage, *choose* to say. Beyond cultural mandates of smiling niceness, leaders in churches are called to speak the truth in love, even when doing so is not a pleasant or comfortable experience for anyone involved. As Schaller put it:

---

[2]Lyle Schaller, as quoted in John P. Chandler, "Churches in a New World: An Interview with Lyle Schaller," *Religious Herald* (November 17, 2005): 4.

The most common expression of the courage to tell the truth is to say, "It ain't workin'." I've had a dozen or two extremely difficult experiences over forty years where a pastor would say to me, "You think my future is with this congregation or not?" The polite thing to say is, "Yes, you can stay here and serve as long as you want, or until something better or more challenging comes along." But to tell the truth is to say, "It ain't workin'."[3]

Vision involves the courage to hear and tell the truth, the whole truth, and nothing but the truth. In a congregation that is not fulfilling its Kingdom potential, this can be painful. It requires what people in the recovery movement dub *rigorous honesty*. For a recovering addict, rigorous honesty might not only mean confessing substance abuse, but also offering full disclosure of temptations, weaknesses, and "slips."

Many leaders in the congregations I work with have a very clear sense of God's calling for their church. They have an equally clear sense of the competing agendas of others in the congregation, and the high cost of bumping against those. Perhaps we can learn from conversations with effective practitioners how to speak with courageous honesty. Schaller says that this might mean voicing a painful truth that, in a society that competes for the affection and attention of people, this congregation is no longer making acceptable progress toward its Kingdom calling:

> You've got more competition operating at a higher level than what you did back when you were competitive ten years ago or whenever it was. But now, you are no longer competitive. "Well, we're doing what we always did and it always worked." And I say, "The road that brought you to today is not the road that's going to take you to tomorrow." It takes courage to lead and to say that.[4]

In another instance, courageous honesty might mean rigorous insistence that a congregation is heading in the right direction even in the face of doubters, skeptics, and enemies. We would do well to glean models of conversation from practitioners who demonstrate the courage to be rigorously honest in their communities of faith.

***Opportune and persistent reinforcement.*** Many congregations are neither clear nor honest about who they are attempting to touch and reach. In Virginia Baptist churches, I will often ask churches to show their founding and governing documents. Then I ask for demonstration of how their stated mission is reflected in the current church budget and calendar. Usually there is a marked gap between mission statements about the church's evangelistic purposes and actual current congregational investments reflected in time and money.

---

[3]Ibid., 4.
[4]Ibid., 10.

Leadership involves the ongoing, diligent permeation of vision in the life of the congregation. Attentive visionaries apply consistent influence over time so that the clear, honest vision of the church is reflected in its daily practices. Once a church identifies its core Kingdom values, it is a leader's role to make the "walk" accountable to the "talk."

Of course, this ongoing task of persistent vision reinforcement happens in formal channels such as sermons and official vision-casting experiences (such as strategy retreats). But effective practitioners never miss an opportunity to give voice to the congregation's core Kingdom assignment. Vision takes root in hallway conversations, over coffee, and during "the meeting after the meeting." Effective leaders never miss an open window for vision expression or enhancement. They are prepared to give a stump speech or to hear one. We will watch for how effective practitioners look for and capitalize on planned and unplanned vision opportunities.

## Leadership

Leadership is such a broadband term that it can die the death of thousand qualifications and definitions. For our purposes, leadership at the pinch-point of a congregation's longing toward a more Kingdom-sized scope of ministry has to do with the willingness to stand in the crossfire of competing visions and agendas. My Virginia Baptist conversations about leadership are often starkly minimalist: "How can a leader with the right vision hang in there long enough, amidst severe pressure, to have lasting impact on the lived-out direction of the church?"

We talk about surviving long enough to lead. That is not a glitzy or urbane picture of leadership. But in a commonwealth where the average Virginia Baptist pastor lasts only four years in a congregation, it is a necessary one. It is difficult to lead when a large portion of a ministry is occupied with getting to know, being in conflict with, and then getting ready to leave a congregation!

Many leaders are occupied with how to deal with dissent appropriately. Because every leader faces opposition, I believe we would greatly benefit from overhearing how effective practitioners deflect or absorb the inevitable critique of vision "point leaders." What we might look to learn about leadership in our conversations can be summarized as follows.

***The ability to process criticism.*** Church leaders are subjected to a mind-boggling volume of Monday-morning quarterbacking. I once asked a church architect about why there were so many church arguments about the selection of the color and style of the carpet. He replied that, while very few people understood technical issues related to roof trusses, nearly every person in the church got up in the morning, stood in front of a mirror, and decided that they knew what looked good: "Everyone is an expert in what looks good!" By the same token, people who have extensive experience *attending* church sometimes automatically assume that they have great expertise *leading* church. While flying as a passenger in a jet doesn't necessarily mean that you know how to pilot one, that does not stop many from offering critique to those in the cockpit.

Criticism of church leaders can range from the merely annoying to soul-withering evil to life-transforming breakthrough. Some criticism of church leaders comes from the pit of hell, voiced by falsely pious clergy-killers who intend to maim, kill, and destroy. Given Jesus' warning about wolves in sheep's clothing, church settings may be thick with these critics. The biblical message to such wolves is in David's response to those who suggested an attack on King Saul: "The LORD forbid that I should do this thing unto my master, the LORD's anointed, to stretch forth mine hand against him" (1 Sam. 24:6, KJV).

Other criticism may be gentle rebuke or prophetic challenge. Confuse the intent of criticism and you may imperil your leadership in that congregation. It is possible to be so distracted, wounded, or victimized by criticism that one's ministry is fatally compromised. It is also possible to be so insulated from the confrontational words of others that you find yourself naked in the public square, unable to hear that "the emperor has no clothes."

Herein lies what may separate effective from ineffective courageous leaders: the ability to filter the nature, intent, and content of the criticism, and then move forward toward the Kingdom vision. It will be instructive to listen to how our practitioners process criticism.

***Gaining long tenure.*** A corollary to the issue of criticism has to do with how long leaders are able to remain in their role. Charles Arn has done interesting research a congregation's willingness to follow the change initiatives of a pastor.[5]

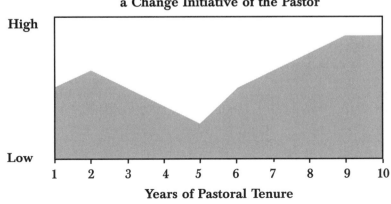

**Willingness of a Congregation to Follow
a Change Initiative of the Pastor**

High

Low

1  2  3  4  5  6  7  8  9  10

**Years of Pastoral Tenure**

---

[5]Charles Arn, *How to Start a New Service: Your Church Can Reach New People* (Baker Book House, 1997), 54.

Based on this insightful graph, my working hypothesis among Virginia Baptist church leaders has been that congregations resist bold transition proposals once they believe the pastor is going to ditch them for another ministry. Given that the average tenure of pastors in Virginia is around four years, this is not an unreasonable suspicion. Perhaps it is a self-fulfilling prophecy. Whether it is or not, what is clear is that leaders have to remain in a ministry setting long enough to garner congregational trust, relationship, and cooperation necessary to walk together toward full Kingdom potential.

Leaders who process criticism appropriately are able to remain in their place of service. The congregation sees them as wise and seasoned guides. They accumulate "relationship capital" on which they are able to "draw" in order to initiate and receive difficult conversations.

None of this is to suggest that leaders cannot be effective quickly. Nor is it to discount the reality that some leaders remain in churches for long tenures because both leader and congregation are too lazy or afraid to challenge a customary relationship. Yet, it suggests a strong correlation between long-tenured leaders and long-term ministry effectiveness. A series of short-term leaders will lead toward long-term ministry ineffectiveness. We should turn an eye toward how long these interviewed practitioners have been in their place of ministry, and be curious as to how that came to pass.

***Capturing life-giving learning opportunities.*** Leaders are able to remain in their ministry setting over the long haul when they find ongoing challenge and fruitfulness. Many are able to see a progression of "chapters" of ministry, or what Henry Blackaby calls "spiritual markers," in a way that calls forth their fullest and most creative engagement.[6]

Such interpretation occurs in the context of learning communities. For some, a learning community might be a cadre of congregational soul mates who help interpret criticism and transform hardship and brokenness into fuel for better leadership. It might be a group of fellow leaders who, out of the experience of authentic community, help the leader interpret life and embolden the leader to act.

A learning community might be a greenhouse, viewing innovative ministry models through the particularities of one's own unique setting. I know of very few effective ministry settings that are slavish clones of another prominent ministry. I know of many congregations in which early-adopter leaders have figured out how to synthesize the best practices of other ministries within their own unique setting and calling in ways that are remarkable.

We will want to watch for what brings joy to effective practitioners' hearts. Amidst often-discouraging negative feedback, long-term leaders find

---

[6]Henry T. Blackaby and Claude V. King, *Experiencing God: Knowing and Doing the Will of God,* workbook ed. (Nashville: Lifeway Resources, 1990).

life-giving encouragement in leadership communities. Seeing where others find sustenance may be a path to help us find our own.

### Structure

For over eleven years, I served as pastor of a rural congregation that grew from seventeen to over four hundred in average weekly worship attendance. I have often since shared that during that time I served four different churches; they just all happened to share the same street address. The congregation at two hundred in attendance was radically different from the congregation at forty in attendance. Moreover, what helped the church move from point "A" to point "B" was often counterproductive in helping it to grow from point "B" to point "C." Heavy personal visitation of members and prospective members when the church averaged thirty in attendance became impossible and inappropriate at three hundred in attendance. In short, I had to unlearn older leadership styles and models of ministry in order to grow into congregational ministry that not only fit our new size and style, but also fit the scope of the ministry that we were being called to become. We truly behave our way into believing, and the only way to grow to a certain size was to "act that larger size" before actually arriving there!

From that experience, I have come to believe that visionary leadership is necessarily lived out in the structural life of the congregation. Some describe the journey from very small to very large church as the transformation from patriarchal/matriarchal to pastoral model, from pastoral to program model, from program to corporate model, and finally from corporate to fractal model. Vision without structural embodiment is simply a bright idea. Leadership without structural incarnation is just purely conceptual. But when vision and leadership begin to manifest themselves in budgets, calendars, schedules, teaching topics, and processes, then transformation becomes possible and evident.

Here are some of the structural lessons we might look to learn from effective practitioners:

***Learning what to release and what to hold onto.*** Pastors, like nurses and social workers, belong to a broader occupational class of what some term "helping professions." Ministry leaders want to impact lives, serve neighbors, and transform communities. This noble urge carries in its bosom an impulse that, left unrecognized, can diminish the very aim it sets out to accomplish. Helpers feel most alive when visibly and recognizably helping. There is nothing wrong with that, in and of itself. The problem arises when leaders become so hooked on doing the helping personally that they do not attend to the less immediate but (long-term) more effective work of equipping others to do the helping. It can be gratifying for the minister to be present personally at every hospital bedside or counseling session. It may be less emotionally gratifying for the "helping leader" to spend time equipping others as counselors and visitors. But unless the leader is willing to release enough of the personal ministry to others, there are unalterable limits as to how much ministry can be accomplished in any one time and place.

Lyle Schaller and Carl George have long distinguished a *shepherd* model of ministry, which insists on personally doing every ministry action, from a *rancher* model of ministry, which insists on seeing to it that every needed ministry is done, whether or not the leader personally does it. Every congregational leader faces tensions about whether to function as the point guard or the coach, the builder or the architect, the tribal chief or the medicine man, the doer of ministry or the equipper for ministry. Effective leaders navigate ever-changing contexts of these tensions. Moving between spoken and unspoken expectations, and in the sometimes shadowy realm of what motivates and drives one's personal ministry, these leaders figure out what they can and cannot do as ministry span of care expands. We should watch for how these leaders determine what to release and what must remain theirs alone.

***Willingness to shed what once worked well but is no longer appropriate.*** This is a restatement of the personal ability described above, now expressed on a corporate, philosophical, or structural level. We will watch some of these effective practitioners wrestle with giving up certain ministry activities that they and/or their congregations had long valued (such as performing weddings or doing hospital visitation). We will see that each led the congregation to give up practices that once held sway but now interfere with what the church envisions becoming.

It is possible to be so married to a ministry practice as to hold onto the practice even when new needs call for new practices. It may be wise for the professional baseball manager to claim that in the playoffs, "We're gonna dance with who brung us." (Interpretation: We will use the same strategies throughout the playoffs that we used to become a playoff team in the first place.) But what if, as Schaller remarked, "The road that brought you to today is not the road that's going to take you to tomorrow"? That same baseball advice turns out to be lousy counsel for ministry leaders. Effective practitioners are willing to abandon ideas, practices, and strategies that resulted in great and visible results at one point in ministry when they come to believe that the same things will not bring fruit in a later point of ministry. It would be a blessing to watch and learn from them how this might be done.

***Thriving within complexity.*** A congregation's size can be a direct reflection of its leaders' abilities to cope and thrive within evolving com-plexity. Leaders with "control issues" can, up to a point, help a congregation move toward fulfilling Kingdom potential. Some high-control leaders pay near-fanatical administrative attention to detail and doggedly insist on full organizational alignment with vision, values, and goals. This, however, seems to conflict with a spirit of releasing ministers and ministries that become much broader than any one leader can manage.

As the church I led began to grow, a dear friend who was there from the earliest stages would frequently drop by for conversation. Carlos would often begin with the greeting, "Hi John. Everything under control?" My stock answer quickly became, "Wrong question!" First of all, it was the wrong question because my ability to control everything (or even many things) was severely limited by experience and competence. Beyond that, it was the wrong question because the goal of control was fundamentally incompatible with the vision of our church as a county-transforming Kingdom movement. If we were to change the face of our community, it would happen because we exploded out of control, not because we were well controlled. I understood Carlos, who came from a corporate management background, and loved his passion for aligning vision and structure. But I also saw and spoke of the need to move our leadership beyond a mechanical controlling of levers and into a more organic model of fertilizing a mustard seed that would grow disproportionately.

Somewhere between sloppy and lazy inattention to detail and hyper-controlling authoritarianism is a sweet spot where leaders are comfortable enough with complexity to let it grow and not manage it down to a smaller level. We would be wise to learn from these conversations the mindset of ministering in escalating complexity.

***Summary***. It is now time to turn to overhearing the practitioner conversations. We will circle back at the end and gather learning about *vision, leadership,* and *structure.* Specifically, we will be attuned to such issues as how leaders:

- Maintain clarity among the clutter of competing visions
- Exhibit courageous, rigorous honesty in congregations
- Persist in opportune reinforcement of vision and values
- Filter criticism appropriately
- Attain sufficient tenure for long-term effectiveness
- Find life-giving learning communities and opportunities
- Learn when, what, and how to release ministry
- Shed favored habits and practices when evolving situations so dictate
- Thrive in ever-growing complexity

We hope to come out with take-away insights on each of these key issues. Such insights sketch the lines of a portrait of courageous church leadership.

# 2

*Interview with* **Bob Russell**
Southeast Christian Church, Louisville, Kentucky
www.southeastchristian.org

# Courageous Span

Until his retirement in June 2006, Bob Russell served as pastor of Southeast Christian Church in Louisville, Kentucky. Southeast Christian is one of the largest churches in the nation, with an average weekly worship attendance of more than eighteen thousand at the time of this writing. (The church has increased by two thousand in average weekly worship attendance since this interview was conducted several years before his retirement.) He is the author of several books, including *When God Builds a Church.*[1] Southeast Christian is remarkable not only for its span of influence and tremendous size but also for the four-decade span of Bob's ministry.

### Here's a Trip-tik™ of things to watch for:
✓ The ongoing buildup of trust between pastor and congregation that accumulated over the years, and what it enabled them to accomplish and risk together
✓ The "steady growth, then spurt" pattern of the church's increasing span of ministry, noting the impact of key events like the call of a pastor, relocation, and moving into a new building
✓ The assessment of the correlation between increasing span of ministry and its corresponding increase in quality

---

[1]Bob Russell, with Rusty Russell, *When God Builds a Church: 10 Principles for Growing a Dynamic Church* (West Monroe, La.: Howard, 2000).

✓ How vision can be spurred on by seeing it in practice in other congregations, and "borrowed" from congregational leaders

✓ The intentional focus on winning, recruiting, and mentoring leaders and administrators

✓ A sense of self-confidence that fosters creativity by enabling pastor and congregational leaders to offer and reject muses on innovation

✓ Ability to "let go" of certain ministry practices as the congregation transitioned to new sizes

✓ Implementing incremental changes as a long-term strategy for increasing ministry span

---

**Chandler:** Bob, could you tell us a little about the Southeast story and some of the trends and growth patterns you've seen while you've been pastor here?

**Russell:** The South Louisville Christian Church started our church in 1962. It had about fifty members who were living in the East End. Seven or eight miles was a long way to drive at that point and that congregation was in the habit of starting new churches. Olin Hay, the minister at that church, asked the people who would be starting the new church to stand. When they stood, he said his heart sank, because standing was his brother-in-law (who was also the choir director), and the organist, and one or two of the key leaders in the church. That's one of the reasons this church has done well–it was started right. It was started with talented, dedicated people. They began meeting in a school, then in a basement of a house.

I came here in 1966. They had a guy preach the first two years who was a church starter, a church planter. When he left they thought, "We have one hundred and twenty-five people, a lot of potential; we ought to be able to persuade somebody with a good track record to come." They came right up to the edge with a couple of really good ministers, but those ministers backed off. They spent a year without a preacher. They said, "Well maybe the Lord is leading us to a younger man." They contacted me. I was twenty-two years old, fresh out of Bible College. I look back now and say, "How in the world did that happen, other than God making it happen?" Anyway, I was twenty-two, came in 1966, they were still meeting in the basement of a house, but they had already started a building. From that, I've been here a few years now.

If you're talking about growth patterns for us, there's been consistent growth over the years–sometimes dramatic, sometimes just a little. But every year, the average worship attendance has increased some degree from the year before. I couldn't say the same about the Sunday school attendance. One year, maybe it was the 1970s, the [attendance] increase was just eleven one year, and twenty-some the next. That wasn't dramatic growth, but there's been consistent growth. But two or three times, there's been dramatic growth, and each time it had to do with a building. When we completed our first building, attendance jumped about a hundred people. Then we relocated in 1987, and in a couple of years' time we increased two thousand people. And then in 1999 we moved into this facility, and in one year's time we jumped almost three thousand people.

**Chandler:** As a twenty-two year old, what sort of vision did you have for the church, and how has that vision evolved?

**Russell:** I was not just twenty-two years old; I was twenty-two and from the country, coming to a city environment. I didn't have much of a vision for the church. I grew up in a church of sixty people. I anticipated that I would probably go back to my home area of Pennsylvania and preach in a country church. God has a sense of humor. I would say we have, for the most part, *reacted* to growth, more than we've *planned* for growth. I have a friend here in this church, Butch Dabney, who is now eighty-some years old. People say, "Butch, when you started this church, did you in your wildest imagination think it would grow to fourteen thousand people?" He responds by saying, "Well, we're a little behind schedule." Butch is hilarious because nobody dreamed that this would happen.

We have tried to teach and preach the Bible and make it as applicable as it can be, ministering to people's needs. We have also responded to the growth that has happened. We had a long-range planning committee about ten years ago, and in about three months time they changed their name to the "short-term crisis committee," because it was just catching up with growth all of the time. We are trying to do better now; we have just completed a strategic plan for the next ten years and it will be interesting to see how that contributes to our future. I'm not saying that's the way most growth should take place, because I think where there's no vision the people perish (Prov. 29:18). But, we have reacted to growth. There has been a willingness on the part of the leadership here to take risks all the time and that's made a big difference. When we had growth, we said, "We need to go to multiple services." Or we had growth, and said, "We need to start shuttling people from a parking lot some distance away," "We need to think about relocating," or "We need to take a big step and have a big fundraiser." They were willing to take those risks. Or, "We'll start Saturday night church." There was that willingness to stretch, in order to accommodate more people. I think that so many times there's not that willingness on the part of church leadership to let that happen, and we get in the way of growth.

**Chandler:** Was there a certain point in which vision began to form in your mind as to what Southeast could do and become?

**Russell:** I just scrambled to stay alive for the first few years. I would go home on Sunday night and say to my wife, "Judy, I might as well resign. That's as good as it's going to get. We could never do any better than that;

this is the peak; it's going to be all downhill from here." And it would keep getting better and better. When we got to be about five hundred people, which was a large church at that time (we're talking mid-seventies or so), I went to a convention in California and visited three different churches that were running probably over two thousand people. One was Los Gatos Christian Church, where a guy named Marvin Reccord was. The others were The Evangelical Free Church, the place where Charles Swindoll was, and Eastside Christian Church in Fullerton, where Ben Merold was. Now, I had always been skeptical of large churches. My wife had taken me to a church that had five hundred people when we were dating and I came away saying, "That's too big, they don't know the pastor, they don't know each other, how could that be a church?" (If you had told me that this was going to happen here, I'd have never believed it.) But at these churches, in 1974, I was stunned by the dedication of these people. A higher percentage of their people carried their Bibles, and heard the sermon. The choir was singing without any music in front of them. They had practiced harder than our choir had, and they were doing more; there was a deeper spiritual thrust in their church than in our church. I realized you don't have to compromise the truth in order to grow; sometimes it's just the opposite.

**Chandler:** So sometimes the larger your church grows, the more it excels, even in the quality of its spiritual life?

**Russell:** Oh, no question. This was a stunner to me. I also said, "You know what, there's nothing that they're doing that we can't do. We're in the Midwest and this is California, but we can do those things." And I came back and I shared what I had seen with our leaders. They didn't say, "Oh, the preacher's gone off and gotten these big ideas, we'll have to squelch him." They were receptive. I have not been a great visionary in this church, but, from the beginning, I was surrounded by lay leaders who encouraged me and wanted me to grow and wanted the church to be what God wanted it to be. From that inception my vision started to get bigger and bigger about church growth.

**Chandler:** Can you talk a little about that process of getting lay leaders on board with this new glimpse of the future you saw for Southeast?

**Russell:** Well, I have been blessed here because I've had those kinds of leaders from the beginning. You asked about what's the easiest part of church growth. The easiest part for me has been leadership training, because I haven't had to do very much of that. For friends who are in churches where they're frustrated, this is frustration number one. They can't get leaders on board with the vision, or they don't have leaders who are true leaders. If someone goes to church two or three times a week and tithes, they're considered a "leader." But the Bible talks about those who are gifted for administration, those who are called to be pastors, and churches really need to win and then to put into positions of leadership those who have leadership skills. Henry Ford was asked, "Who should sing tenor in the quartet?" He says you don't just put anybody in the tenor section; the tenor sings tenor. The person is gifted to do that. Who should lead the church? It should be people with leadership skill. I was blessed when I came here to have people with leadership skills and who had a real dedication and commitment to the cause of Christ.

**Chandler:** What does a church do when its people in leadership roles do not have leadership gifts?

**Russell:** That's a tough situation. First of all, you've got to be patient. The pastor and the lay leaders have to be on the same page for it to happen or you're going to create all kinds of disharmony and not be able to climb the mountain together. Sometimes it takes awhile to get there. So the pastor's got to be in it for the long haul. Second, I think the pastor's got to work at winning some leadership-type people into the church—either converting them to Christ, or looking at the leadership people you've already got and saying, "We need you!" and trying to deepen these people.

However, the most effective technique that I've seen in winning people over is for the preacher *not* to go to seminars or church growth conventions by himself! So many times he goes, he comes back, he's fired up, he's got ideas...and it serves as a point of alienation. When he goes by himself, he needs to come back and be quiet, be patient. He needs to take key leaders with him, let them see, let them talk, and let them get fired up when they come back. I think leadership is like a magnet. With a magnet you can stay just a little bit ahead and you'll draw...You get too far ahead, they drop out. If they sense your enthusiasm and your goals are too far beyond what their goals are, you'll alienate them. I've got two friends right now who have been terminated from their positions, though their churches were growing and doing well. The leaders of those churches said, "We just don't share your vision; your goals for church make us feel uncomfortable." So a preacher has to sense how far ahead his vision is from that of his key leaders. If it's too far ahead, he's got to slow down; he's got to gear it down until he gets them on the same page. The best way I see to get them on the same page is to take them with you somewhere that is the next level or two levels ahead of where they are. If you go someplace that's too big, that's too dramatically different, they're going to be frightened by that.

**Chandler:** Talk about a time when you got out too far ahead of the "magnetic range" of your folk. What happened, how did you get back in range, and what leadership lessons did you learn?

**Russell:** Well, let me speak to the opposite first. There have been times when their vision has been bigger than mine. For example, we had a building committee on our first relocation project—we were in a building that seated five hundred—and I said to that building committee, "I would like for our building to seat fifteen hundred. With two services, we could have three thousand in the morning. But I'm concerned about Wednesday night and Sunday night; if it gets much bigger than fifteen hundred, we're going to rattle around in there. I just want fifteen hundred people." The building committee, chaired by an elder who is a good friend of mine, said to me, "Your vision is too small. You preach; we'll build the building. We're going to build this building to seat twenty-five hundred." They were far ahead of me. I mumbled and grumbled, but I liked it at the same time. I liked the fact that I was not the one pulling them out there. I would say that more times their vision has been bigger than mine.

There have been some ideas that I've had that have been screwy and that were wrong. I had an idea for Sunday school one time—I thought that quality in Sunday school is what we needed—so we said let's have all of our teachers specialize in a thirteen-week series and let's rotate the teachers. This doctor who specializes in evolution versus creation will come into this class, and they'll just gobble it up and then move on. It was disastrous in our Sunday school, which is more fellowship than an identification with the teacher, who is the "pastor" for that class. I had to say, "I made a mistake here; my idea didn't work."

When we moved out here, we had this huge parking lot. My vision for the parking lot was, "You know what? It is a long way from one end of the parking lot to the front door. We'd better have some way of shuttling people." I said, "Let's buy thirty of these golf carts that seat six or eight people and drive people—see, your reaction [*Chandler laughs*] is the same as our elders' was—I said, "Let's pick people up in golf carts and let's transport them to the front door." They said, "Who's going to drive the golf carts?" I said, "That would be a great role for teenagers; teenagers would love to do that." They laughed me out of the door. So when my ideas get screwy, I have these lay leaders who will say to me, "That's a goofball idea." If I have five ideas, I want them to be able to shoot four of them down. I try to create the atmosphere where they can say no to me, they can tell me the truth, and I'm not threatened by it. I don't put my head down, I don't pout, I don't go out of the meeting and refuse to speak to guys or bad-mouth guys because they don't go along with my idea. I don't want to be out there by myself; I want the input from those people. Sometimes I've disagreed with them and later they were proven wrong. And sometimes I've disagreed with them and later they were proven right. But when we come out of there, I want us all to be on the same page. So I feel like they can say what they want to say and they don't have to worry about hurting Bob's feelings; that's been one of the strengths of the harmony of our meetings. I can have Jack Coffey, who's an elder and a good friend of mine, look at me in the eye and say, "That's the dumbest idea I've ever heard you give." And I'll say, "No, it's not, Jack," and we'll still walk out of there saying, "Where does everyone want to eat?"

**Chandler:** So when I'm willing to admit that I may be wrong, and create a climate where people can tell me I'm wrong, and where I develop a culture where leaders can be cultivated or brought on board alongside people who may be in leadership roles but may not have leadership gifts, I can eventually begin to reshape...

**Russell:** I think that's a great summary, and I would add one thing. These leaders have to feel like they are leading. It's not just the preacher who is leading. They're out there on the point, with the preacher; we're doing this together. If you've got five or six key people with leadership skills and you're on the same team, you're going to have eight or ten in that same group who maybe aren't as strong, but they're good secondary-level people. They are good followers, and they will help you to follow through...Then you've got a good team. But there's never this feeling of, "Here's Bob Russell and here's three or four guys around him and they're following his lead and they're strong and they're 'yes' people." We're doing this thing together.

**Chandler:** What have you had to let go of as a leader that's been hard for you to let go of?

**Russell:** I have a list! I've had to let go of a lot. I started here as a pastor, my model for ministry is a pastor. So I had to let go of hospital visits, and I let go of them slowly. We finally got an associate and instead of me going four times a week, I'd go twice. And then we got two associates and I'd go just once and eventually I hardly ever go to the hospital anymore. I let go of almost all committee meetings; it's an old thing called delegation: you can stop and tie their shoe or you can teach them to tie their own shoe and let them go tie it. I let go of participation in a lot of extracurricular activities of the church, like camps and athletic events.

Two other things I've released: I've released a lot of preaching and teaching responsibilities. That's the hardest thing for preachers to release, that pulpit. Right now, we have a preaching associate who preaches a third of the time. We also have guest speakers on Wednesday nights as well as Sunday morning. It's healthy for me: I love those weeks when I don't have that sermon hanging over my head. I love it until it gets to be service time...and then I wish I were preaching. It's also healthy for the congregation—they're hearing somebody else; they're not hearing me all the time. I don't know how you can have a long ministry when you're up all the time. When I relinquished a lot of preaching responsibilities, I relinquished a lot of worship leadership. I don't get up and make announcements anymore; most of the time I don't get up until it's time for me to preach. I've relinquished planning worship. Most of the time I go to worship and I don't know what's going on except a brief perusal of what's on the text sheet.

**Chandler:** Do you give sermon themes to a worship committee and they'll design a service around that?

**Russell:** Yes. Another thing I learned was saying no to individual requests. I still have people come up and say, "Will you go to bat for me?" I want to say yes; I love pleasing people; I have a hard time saying no; but

I've had to learn to say no to people. I heard John MacArthur say one time that if he said yes to an hour's counseling on Thursday to a couple, he just said no to eight thousand people he was going to preach to on the weekend. I had to adjust my thinking. So one of the things I cut out was all marital counseling. Praise God, I don't do any more marital counseling. I can do it adequately, but nothing drained me like that; it was not a passion of mine. Even before we had a counseling staff, I learned to give referrals, even to people who say, "I've got to talk to you, can we see you about this marriage?" I learned to say to people, "I want you to have the best counseling you can get and I'm not it. I have a friend who is a counselor and I'm going to give you his name. I'll talk with him about the situation; I'm going to stay in touch with him about the situation; I want you to go to him." I am surprised at how receptive people were to that. But it's tough learning to say no.

**Chandler:** A number of pastors of congregations of one hundred would say, "But I don't have someone to whom I can hand off worship planning or marital counseling or hospital visitation. How do you get started with delegating ministry?"

**Russell:** I've been in that church of one hundred. I understand that these pastors wear many hats, and there's an awesome amount of pressure on them. And to some degree that's true—there's too much expected of them. But I also think, looking back, there are people in the church who are gifted to do those things. If we would go to them and say, "You know, I go to the hospital three times a week, and I would like for you to go once or twice in my place. Would you be willing to do that? And here's what I want you to do…" And then we go to the church and say, "I want you to know the decision that we've made," and that you've gone to the leaders and the leaders agree. Not so much is expected of the preacher when you've got someone in the church who can actually sit and talk with people about marital problems, and they are as qualified as you are. Almost every preacher is way out of his league, pretending something that isn't real, if he thinks he's a marital counselor. You've got people to whom you can say, "Would you be willing to counsel with people if I could channel them to you?" They would be willing to do that. I think the resources will often be available in a small church. Many times we hold on to those responsibilities because it makes us feel needed.

The genius of this church right now is the involvement of the laypeople. We don't have a program where preachers go to visit in the hospital. We do have people in the church who love to go visit in the hospital; that's what they're gifted to do. So when somebody goes, people used to say, "Bob, when I was in the hospital, you were really good to me." Now people say, "Bob, I was in the hospital for a week and a half"—and I kind of still brace myself for the "Where were you?"—"and *the church* was really good to me." And they'll tell me, "When those people from church come by, they're not in a hurry, they don't just try to leave a card—'Sorry, you're sleeping'—they really want to be there." We do the same thing with a lot of our counseling sessions. We have a care ministry where if you've been through a particular problem, you're matched up with somebody who had a similar problem. You know who's happiest? The people who serve in those capacities. Now in some ways it hurts the preacher, because all of a sudden the whole world isn't revolving around you.

**Chandler:** If you have a codependent bone in your body, you feel that ache in it.

**Russell:** That's exactly right. One year, I did thirty-seven weddings. You know, that's a lot of weekends. I was maxed out and thought, "I can't do this many." I went to my secretary, Barbara, and said, "Next year, I'm going to do just fifteen weddings—first come, first served. You channel the others to other people and staff people." Well, it went pretty well...until one Saturday morning, I was walking through the church, and they were setting up for a wedding. I asked the custodian, "Who's getting married?" He told me, and I was crushed, because it was a family I'm really close to. I said, "Barbara, I know I made this rule, fifteen, but if someone like that asks me, make an exception." She replied, "They didn't ask for you!" [*laughter*] That hurts. You're saying, "It's not all about me." The preacher has to be willing to get ego out of it, whether in a church of one hundred or a church of three thousand.

**Chandler:** Has there been anything that you let go of prematurely? Any mistakes that you've made and lessons you could share from your experience?

**Russell:** I backed off of leadership of the staff too early. When we would have staff meetings, I'd have somebody else on the leadership team run the staff meetings. I did that for about a year, and there was this sense of aimlessness or disorientation on staff. Several key people on the staff said, "Bob, we need you up front; it's okay to relinquish some of those things, but when it comes to a building program, there are some treacherous waters here, and we need your up-front presence in the staff meeting. We'll prepare the agenda, but you stand up front, because there's a sense of being without a leader."

**Chandler:** Where are you most "at home" as a leader? On the flip side, what areas of being a lead pastor are still the "pay the rent" areas that you have to do? They may not be your passion or your calling but you still have to do them. In other words, where are you happiest, and where are you most workmanlike?

**Russell:** I'm happiest at two extremes. I'm happiest in the small leadership group of six or eight, where I know the agenda that is being set, the tone that is being set, where I can let my hair down and be completely unguarded, and if I want to gripe a little bit, I can gripe a little bit, and if I want to praise, I can praise…without having to worry about it getting out and being multiplied three times more than its significance. And then I'm happy in front of the whole congregation, where if we have a mountain to climb, I can get up and I'm fired up, because I sense that these people believe in me because of the long-term pastorate. They feel confidence in me because I've been there before. I can say, "This is what we're going to do; we're on the same page; this is where we're going to go." I feel comfortable doing that.

This sounds really egotistical: I'm not happy in meetings I'm not leading. I get impatient, unless they're really well led; then I'm okay. But if we're lingering and lingering and hashing and rehashing…I try to stay out of those meetings. I'm not as effective as I would like to be with the large staff on retreat. Every year we have a staff retreat, and I have to get up and address the staff. When it's done, I'm glad I did it. Last month it was "Ten Commandments to a staff member of Southeast Christian Church." But I'm not as comfortable in that setting. I can't tell you why.

**Chandler:** In a way you're most comfortable in the cell size and the celebration size; but you're not as comfortable in that middle congregation-size group.

**Russell:** I wish I could analyze myself and say what it is…but that's what it is.

**Chandler:** Many North American churches are very traditional, not only in the sense of theology, but they have a sense of congregational history and heritage. While that provides a certain kind of rootedness for the church, it also makes change very slow. What kinds of encouraging words would you say to pastors and lay leaders in very slow-moving churches to help them work where God is working and reach kinds of people they have not reached before?

**Russell:** First, I don't think it's a gimmick that's going to reach people. Sometimes we go to a place that is reaching people by the hundreds. We think it's because they don't sing hymns or because they have a band and they don't have an organ. Those may be contributing factors. But probably the reason they're growing is something significant other than that. Maybe they are in an area that is ripe for receiving the seed of the gospel, and it's going to grow thirty, sixty, or one hundred-fold. Other areas can be pretty hard ground. Or maybe they are growing because of *excellence.* Many times it is a commitment to excellence more than it is a methodology. Whatever you're doing, do it with excellence. If you're singing traditional hymns, do it with excellence. You still have that opportunity to get up there and preach; do that with excellence. I still think preaching is so important. That's your opportunity to feed people; people sit there and listen to the word of God. If that is done with excellence, you can make a lot of mistakes in other areas.

I think you have to make changes slowly in a traditional church. I once heard Fred Craddock say, "You don't rearrange the furniture in the room of a disoriented person." People are disoriented today. They want some stability in their lives. If everything is changing and decaying around them, and if they come to church and all of a sudden they have nothing to hold on to there, they're real frightened. If you're going to make changes, choose your battles carefully and communicate as clearly as you can. "This is what we're doing, this is why, this where we're going; how do you feel about it?" Be really open. There are several times I've gotten up in front of the church and said, "We're going to try something different today, I'm not sure I like it, but let's try it and see how it goes. I'd like your feedback afterwards, too." And people settled in a little bit, as opposed to abruptly dropping something on them.

Let me give you an example. Our music guys went to some place and heard the big band sound in Christian music. They thought to themselves, this is great! We love this sound, young people love this sound, and the older people who grew up with Glenn Miller will love this sound. They got a big band together, did three or four numbers (one of which was "Amazing Grace"–you could hardly tell it was "Amazing Grace," but it was "Amazing Grace"). They didn't say anything to anyone. They just decided they were going to play for ten or fifteen minutes before the service started on Sunday morning. People came in and the big band sound is up there playing swing…and you've never heard such a stir. I mean, people were saying, "Are we at Southeast Bar or what?" They got so many calls and letters that you wouldn't believe it. So we had to get up and say, "You know, folks, we made a mistake with the big band sound. We thought you'd like it, but some of you must have grown up in bars because that's immediately your association with it." And they'd laugh. But we had to say, "You know, we didn't communicate that well. We're not saying it will never come back, but if it does, we'll tell you so you can brace yourself for it." We probably won't do three numbers at once. We rearranged the furniture in the room of a disoriented person and we made a mistake. But when we say in advance, "We're going to make a time change here, we're going to do something different, we're going to have this interview, we're going to have this video clip today; we don't intend to do this every week, y'all settle down!" If they know that you're sensitive to their feelings as opposed to coming in like a steamroller, they'll put down the armor. So make the change slowly, one by one, and do it well."

## Reflecting on the Trip: Questions for Continuing the Conversation

1. Called at age twenty-two, Bob has been able to lead Southeast for so long because he was so young when he started. What trade-offs and risks must a congregation assume when calling a "green" minister?

2. Bob was surprised at how a very large and growing church could attain superior spiritual quality in its congregational life. What factors in growth accentuate a congregation's spiritual life? What factors compromise that quality? How can leaders lead so that an increasing span of ministry parlays strengths unattainable at smaller sizes?

3. What can we learn about the intentional effort to identify, equip, and deploy people with the spiritual gifts of leadership and administration? Why focus on those particular gifts?

4. Beyond taking people with you to best-practice churches and seminars, how does one go about recruiting and mentoring people who will contribute heavily to the "vision-quotient" of the church?

5. What enables a pastor to invite honest feedback and input without being badly bruised by it on a personal level? How can leaders foster atmospheres of honesty and innovation without free dialogue degenerating into personal attack?

6. How can the pastor effectively share the preaching task in ways that engender the vitality of both pastor and congregation?

7. What can we learn from the counsel to make changes in your church slowly, one by one, and with excellence?

*Interview with* **Fred Craddock**
Cherry Log Christian Church, Cherry Log, Georgia
www.craddockcenter.org or www.clccdoc.org

# Courageous Conversing

After a distinguished career as professor and author, Fred Craddock served for several years as the first pastor of Cherry Log Christian Church. As worship attendance in the burgeoning church approached three hundred, he re-retired and continues to serve actively in the congregation, and also at the Craddock Center, a ministry dedicated to Appalachian children. Cherry Log Christian Church is an example of a vital medium-sized church; its leadership faces challenges typical to the vast majority of North American congregations.

**Here's a Trip-tik™ of things to watch for:**
✓ A model of pastoral leadership that "catches up" with where God's people are already moving
✓ The indispensable "leadership capital" that can be accumulated only through the leader's ongoing relationship with people
✓ The place of preaching as part of a larger conversation about leadership, and the necessity of shaping a traditionally one-way medium into dialogical form
✓ The attention to a sense of "calling" and "giftedness" as means of discerning fit and tenure with a particular congregation
✓ How the concept of "staying in my leaving and leaving in my staying" might enable leaders to be appropriately invested in the mission and calling of a particular ministerial setting

✓ How personal and spiritual issues such as envy or competition
   inevitably manifest themselves in congregational settings

---

**Chandler:** How did you become minister at Cherry Log after years of teaching, preaching, and serving as a guest preacher around the country?

**Craddock:** Let me say first that I did not intend that. We moved to the mountains because we loved the setting and I had retired from Emory. Second, I wanted to hold workshops for bi-vocational ministers in southern Appalachia. There are many of them. I wanted to go to them, on an ecumenical basis, on their own turf, and talk with them about preaching. I have been doing that about ten to twelve times a year. When we moved to the mountains, we learned that it was a long way to a local Disciples of Christ congregation. We were worshiping in Methodist churches, Baptist churches, and I was gone most Sundays. But then some Disciples folk said, "Why don't you hold a service with your own denomination in the area?" I said, "I'm a tired and retired seminary professor. I have no church and no place. Then a minister who had been dis-fellowshiped from the *a capella* Church of Christ offered me the use of a little pavilion he owned near a lake. I said, "What will it hold?" "Fifty people, maybe." There were no seats, no pulpit, and no communion table. But people got busy. Borrowed chairs, borrowed Bibles, borrowed tables. Made a little lectern. We held a service. I thought it would be a one-time thing. We did it on Labor Day weekend, 1996. Well-attended, good spirit; they said, "Let's do this again." So six week later, we did it again. They said, "Do it again," and we had a Thanksgiving service. We also had a Christmas Eve service. In January 1997, some of the people who had gotten fascinated with this open, ecumenical service said, "Why don't we meet every Sunday?" I said, "I have a lot of commitments; I can't be here." They responded, "We'll get someone else when you're not here." So I began to teach and preach as often as I was there. Easter of 1997, they said, "We're going to form a church," and opened a charter with fourteen people. A year later had eighty-four. Started talking about building a building. I said, "Wait for me, I'm your leader!" These are strong people with strong church background. It moved along rapidly. They put up a beautiful log church that will seat about one hundred fifty. Membership grew. Baptized in the river. It got to the point that it was obvious that they needed a real minister and not a retired seminary professor. Pastors are called on to do things I was not trained to do. It had been a long time since I was in seminary; I wasn't going to go back to school to be a pastor. But I stayed with it for about six years. Its success ran me away. So they now have a young man from Virginia doing a good job. Just broke ground for a new building and have a membership of about two hundred seventy-five, high percentage attendance, and good participation. My wife and I worship there. I didn't intend it, but I'm glad to have been a part of it. It made a difference in my preaching.

**Chandler**: You've often said that the best preaching happens in local churches from local pastors. Why do you say that, and how was that true in your own experience?

**Craddock:** Well, it was true in my own experience for two reasons. One is the pastor knows the people in a variety of reality situations. A guest preacher comes in and makes a speech, hopes that it will be appropriate to somebody, but never has the satisfaction of knowing. Not having any feedback, not having any follow-up conversations. It's just a blurb on the screen. It may be a good speech; it may not be. But the pastor knows the people and can temper the wind to the shorn lamb and is still there on Monday and Tuesday and Wednesday and Thursday to get feedback. A sermon on the local level, by a pastor, is part of a larger conversation. That conversation goes on and on in a hospital, over coffee, in the committee, and in the community. And it's just a complete thing. Second, it's the appropriateness of it. It's appropriate because you have the cumulative effect of this conversation. And conversation means they can talk back. They don't talk back to the guest speaker unless they just go out in a mad fury. Besides that, I would have to say that the discipline of speaking to the same people every week raised the level and the quality of my preaching. My wife agrees.

**Chandler:** You used up your bag of tricks pretty quickly?

**Craddock:** Exactly. Now you are speaking to occasions, to particular people. You close your eyes and know where every one of them will be seated. Notice when someone's absent. Notice visitors. It quickens your preaching.

**Chandler:** Being in a local congregation means there are all sorts of leadership subtexts in your preaching. So your preaching is not an event in and of itself, but becomes a part of your larger leadership in the lives of people you know and care about.

**Craddock:** That's right. You can take the recording of your preaching to a hospital. Play it bedside: "You thought you were going to get out of this, but I caught you, so here it is!" They like to be part of the conversation, too. You mentioned subtexts. You can make allusions when you're the pastor; allusions to things local, things joyous and sad, and things that have just occurred. The guest preacher cannot. Even if he or she knew, he or she couldn't do it—they don't have the credentials of the local pastor. It's sort of like if you had a nickname and a stranger used it. You're like, "You have no right to use that; that's for the inner circle." That's the way it is with preaching as part of local church leadership.

**Chandler:** You said that your church grew to a certain level and then it "got away from you," and it was time to step down. Can you elaborate?

**Craddock:** Well, I had made a commitment to hold these workshops for bi-vocational ministers, and I was doing it; it took a lot of my time because I went to them: eastern Kentucky, eastern Tennessee, southwestern Virginia, North Carolina, and north Georgia. I was traveling and spending time with them and didn't want to cut that off and say, "Sorry fellows, but I have a church going now." I intended to go up with these bi-vocational pastors; I didn't intend that church. I don't minimize the church; it's just that it was not my intention, and I was not going to let that bump the other off the calendar.

**Chandler:** You had a clear sense of your calling and, in a sense, what the church became was not it.

**Craddock:** Yes, that's right. It was not it.

**Chandler:** Do you have a word from your experience for pastors where either they or their churches grow to a place where their sense of calling, or the level of their ability to lead, changes and no longer fits?

**Craddock:** Yes, I would like for the relationship between pastors and congregations to be open and free. I would like to sustain a conversation as to whether I am still the one to be the pastor here. There are some very good pastors who could not exercise their gifts if their congregations would grow to over two hundred people. They need to become more C.E.O., more administrative, more this and that, and that's not their gift. Somebody else has those gifts. There are gifted people who can handle a larger church. Some, just as gifted, can handle smaller ones. We should assess every year or so, "Am I the right person still?" It's not a matter of resigning or being fired. Out of the conversation may come, "This is not what I came here to do, thank you very much for the experience."

**Chandler:** So some people have the potential to be a full-flowering dogwood, some have the potential to be a full-flowering oak, and there's no judgment in that, but a matter of the matching of the calling and gifting of that pastor with those of the congregation and the community it is trying to reach.

**Craddock:** That's right; exactly, exactly. There's some pain in leaving, but there's pain in staying, too. Do I change my fundamental commitment in order to stay here? Or do I stick with what I believe God gave me gifts to do? Perhaps that's to be somewhere else. "Thank you, I've enjoyed my chapter here, this trip of three or four years, whatever, but I must go."

**Chandler:** How do ministers cope with the pain of staying or the pain of leaving?

**Craddock:** It's very difficult, but it seems to me that if a minister would write on their desk, "There is always going in my staying, and staying in my going," then that would help. Keep enough intimate distance—keep the intimacy, keep the distance—so that it's not the end of the world to stay, it's not the end of the world to go. Where I have taught, I have had that feeling. I enjoyed very much my years of teaching at Emory in Atlanta. But I was not so deeply enmeshed in that where I said, "If something happens to this, I would just shoot myself." It was a piece of a larger picture.

**Chandler:** "Whether I come and see you or am absent and hear about you, I will know that you are standing firm in one spirit and striving for the faith of the gospel" (Phil. 1:27).

**Craddock:** That's right.

**Chandler:** So ministry leadership is being able to engage on a substantial level in a particular place, but not being so tied up or enmeshed in that one place that your whole calling can *only* be expressed with these people in this place.

**Craddock:** Yes. There has to be that freedom. It's not cool or aloof—"I don't want to get close to you"—but it's rethinking every week who I am and what my identity is, and my relationship to these particular people. Is my identity only in this congregation, or do I have an identity in Christ without it? Once that freedom is clear, the church is healthier, and I am healthier. Both can survive without the other. It gives us freedom really to enjoy each other.

**Chandler:** What role might courage from the leader play in the overall health, growth, and vitality of the congregation? What would courage look like from a pastoral standpoint?

**Craddock:** From a pastoral standpoint, I think courage might look like engagement with the congregation on a level playing field. That is, I have conversations with the congregations at times other than from the pulpit. The pulpit is always bully pulpit. From the pulpit, I have a kind of home-field advantage—a sort of a "no talk back" zone. But when issues locally come up that should engage the mind, activity, and prayer life of the whole church…to have an hour of conversation with the church; the leader just standing down front, entertaining questions and points of view. People need to learn to express with courage. If I have the courage to stand down here and raise a matter, listen to your objections, listen to you in a way that feels the anger of some and support of others, then everybody is growing. If I just "preach on it," then it becomes, "That's what the minister thinks, and I agree or disagree." I never want to put a congregation in that position of just agreeing or disagreeing. There has to be a fuller expression of its *own* life.

**Chandler:** Maybe the most courageous preaching is not found simply in the preaching event but in the larger context of conversation between the pastor and people.

**Craddock:** Precisely. And you can handle very controversial matters if you as leader are on the floor, level with the people, and they can talk back. If they can't talk back, you trigger things. People feel like all they can do is quit, give their pledge, or move to another church. Those are not healthy alternatives.

**Chandler:** How might a good leader start that conversation?

**Craddock:** I tried it after worship, after a sermon. But I had already expressed myself so fully in the sermon that it became a simple matter of agreeing or disagreeing. So the way I did it was to request the adult Sunday school hour before worship. We would pull the adults together for an hour, and they would know ahead of time what the conversation was to be about. That was before the sermon. Sometimes it ended in such a way that I really had to shift gears to get ready for worship—but so did they. I had these sorts of meetings or conversations regularly. If you call the meetings only for controversial matters, the congregation will make everything controversial; that's the pattern that's set. So sometimes you get them together because something grand has happened. Sometimes you do it because we need to discuss how we are going to respond to Hurricane Katrina. Sometimes we are going to measure a whole new spurt of growth and ask, "What is really happening here? We didn't do this." Talk about good and bad things. Churches have those lists and moments of joys and concerns, but too few of them celebrate any joys. So talk about those joys together. Then you have a larger context in which to discuss the painful.

**Chandler:** So create conversations that are forums for discernment and wisdom, and these will form the relationship out of which preaching and leadership can be courageous, because it's connected.

**Craddock:** That's right, it's connected. And you can make allusions to previous conversations. Now, some of your members weren't in on the other conversations; that will always be true. But it makes those who *were* there glad they were there, and those who weren't there think, "Maybe next time I ought to go." So I don't allow myself to be silenced by the absence of some people. You can feed off of that conversation in your preaching. "As we talking about last Sunday morning…" You can say things about it.

**Chandler:** This idea of facilitating congregational conversations strikes me as a wise model until the church moves beyond its accustomed size. Suddenly that requires different ingenuity or intentionality or gifts—to lead congregational conversations in a church that has grown to a new size.

**Craddock:** It's very difficult. I have never been pastor of a very large church but have been present to see how it was done. Large-church leaders almost always learn to chop it into smaller groups, age-wise, experience-wise, or labor-wise. Can't do it all in one lump.

**Chandler:** Once the congregation reaches a certain level of complexity, then leadership is about continuing to have these conversations, but figuring out how to do contexts for courage in new ways.

**Craddock:** Right. A woman with whom I talked recently talked about her minister; she belongs to a very large church. I said, "I heard he was ill." She said, "He is?" I said, "I was going to ask you about it; he's your minister."

"Well, I've never really spoken to him." "Haven't you shaken hands with him at the door?" "Oh no, he can't shake that many hands." "Then how do you participate?" Well, she's part of a group within it. They create many such groups in the congregation. Perhaps the lead minister circulates to those groups, or perhaps it's done by a staff person or lay leader. But they figure out a whole new strategy for having these conversations. I wouldn't know how to do it.

**Chandler:** Everyone has a certain set of gifts, and some gift sets are better suited for single-forum conversations, some for creating multiple-forum conversations.

**Craddock:** That's quite true.

**Chandler:** From your experience as a local church minister, what word of hope would you offer other local churches and ministers?

**Craddock:** I would remind ministers and churches not to get in the competition circle. "Why does that church down the road have three thousand, and we have three hundred?" "What are they doing and what are we doing?" Both churches at both sizes can be healthy and belong to God. Get rid of envy and competition; be healthy with your own identity. That may not mean to rest and relax simply at your present size, but to define your calling, what you do. Where I was pastor, at Cherry Log, we said, "When we get to three hundred, we will start a new church down the road somewhere, where there needs to be one, and ask some of our members to participate." That was agreed on and is going to happen soon there.

**Chandler:** Getting rid of envy: that implies that the word of hope could be that if leaders and people will deal with core issues of the spirit, such as envy, gluttony, greed, sloth—the deadly sins. Then there is hope to have vital congregational life and to impact the community with the gospel.

**Craddock:** Oh, yes. To say, "We are a full-service church here, with one hundred twenty members." To celebrate that, not to rest there, but to find contentment with God's calling at whatever God-called size. There's my word of hope. My word to denominations would be, "Do not encourage, by the movement and employment of ministers, upward mobility. Separate faithfulness and success in ministry from size. It can get built into ecclesiastical structures if we're not careful. Therefore if I'm in a church of a hundred, I'm not very successful or faithful. That has to be attacked by all levels of the church.

**Chandler:** Somewhere between sloth and contentment is a magical place where the pastor recognizes personal gifts, the congregation is clear on its unique calling, and where there's a match; then there's a blessed church that can be a blessing to its community.

**Craddock:** Oh so true. And we should hope and strive for nothing less.

**Reflecting on the Trip: Questions for Continuing the Conversation**

1. The beginning of Fred's leadership at Cherry Log occurred without deep planning or great fanfare, arising out of an organic sense of what the emerging congregation needed and what he was able to do. How can leaders maintain ongoing wakefulness so as to respond to surprising opportunities to serve?

2. For Fred, leadership is intensely local, rooted in history, ongoing conversations, memory, and shared experiences. Permission to lead emerged out of relational connectedness. What guidelines are there to help leaders balance the pastoral or priestly roles of offering comfort or building relationships with the prophetic roles of stretching people, attending to task, and calling forth more than people might comfortably offer without leadership prompting?

3. How can leaders determine whether their individual "skill set" or "gift mix" matches where a congregation is and where it might be called to go?

4. Leadership in this context was not a one-way monologue but an ongoing dialogue. Beyond talk-back sessions around the preaching and worship experience, what are ways leaders can make sure they are part of a *leadership community*, receiving input and feedback from multiple sources?

5. In what senses should the leader be "friends" with those whom he or she leads? In what ways is the image of friendship inadequate or inappropriate in the leadership context?

6. Fred left this pastorate when he sensed that the congregation had grown to a place where his primary gifting and calling no longer "fit" for that role, but was best utilized in another context. What are some markers that can help congregational leaders discern when it is time to end a particular chapter in ministry?

## 4

*Interview with* **David Chadwick**
Forest Hill Church, Charlotte, North Carolina
www.foresthhill.org

# Courageous Repositioning

David Chadwick has been pastor of Forest Hill Church since 1980. During his tenure, the church has grown from an average attendance of one hundred and eighty to over three thousand, and has planted several other churches and a video venue. A former basketball player at the University of North Carolina under one of the greatest coaches in college history, David used that experience as a springboard for writing *The 12 Leadership Lessons of Dean Smith.*[1]

## Here's a Trip-tik™ of things to watch for:
✓ Candor about how Chadwick's personal strengths were dangerous to himself and others in the congregation at points
✓ How self-awareness and intuition can be wise prompters and guides for leadership conversations
✓ How Chadwick learned the difference between receiving verbal assent and wholehearted buy-in from other congregational leaders
✓ The key distinctions between transfer and conversion growth and how they impact the climate of leadership and vision
✓ Departures of members as catalysts for unease, truth, and freedom

---

[1]Dean Smith with David Chadwick, *The 12 Leadership Lessons of Dean Smith* (New York: Total Sports Illustrated, 1999).

✓ How a pastor both sets and meets expectations for new and existing people in the congregation

---

**Chandler**: David, can you talk a bit about what led you as a pastor and leader to revamp the direction of Forest Hill in the 1990s?

**Chadwick**: I had been here about eleven years at that point. The one and only time I considered a call to another place occurred at that time. It was a big, five thousand member church that had just bought one hundred thirty acres. It seemed like the perfect thing to do if you're moving up the ladder. Marilyn, my wife, went up there and looked at it. We even had our house painted, thinking that this is what God was doing. But after flying there the second time, both of us, for some unknown reason, began to feel ill at ease about going. We couldn't figure out why, but it persisted. So I told the pulpit committee that I'd pray about it and tell them in a week. At the end of the week, I didn't have any peace. I've always said that's the way you should make a decision, with the peace of the Lord. I didn't feel it, so I called them back and said "no." Then I went to prayer, saying, "What in the world is going on here?"

I think what the Lord communicated to me during that season of prayer was that Forest Hill was a loose-knit confederacy, held together by my personality. I'm a fairly gregarious, open kind of person with a people-pleasing streak. So I had invited into this church in my eleven years successful growth; we had grown from one hundred eighty in worship to over one thousand, so we'd had success in growth. But the people who had come in were charismatics to whom I'd said, "Come in, we love the Holy Spirit here." And evangelicals, who loved the Word of God—and I'm a fairly good expositor—so we said, "Welcome, we preach the Word here." And mainline people who were here because we had a heart for social action. (Note: The church had been part of the Presbyterian Church of the United States of America, but moved into the Evangelical Presbyterian Church; in 2005, it left the EPC.) So we had three different groups of people here. I realized that they were held together by my warm and engaging personality, even though they didn't agree on a whole lot. I think what the Lord said to my heart was that if I'd left at that point, those three groups would have warred for the soul of Forest Hill. That's when I really entered into a deep season of prayer, and came to understand Philippians 2:2, which says we're "united in one purpose." What should unite a church is not the pastor. It's not the music. What should unite a church is its vision. Those people committed to the vision, even though they might have different nuances—charismatic, evangelical, mainline—will be together through the common vision. So I went to the Lord again and said, "Where do I go from here?" And God's answer was, "Where do you want to go?"

I said, "Lord, my heart is for evangelism; it's for lost people, people who've given up on church, who don't go to church." It was one of those, "Aha!" moments where the Lord said, "Well..."

**Chandler**: "Can you do that in Charlotte?"

**Chadwick**: Yes. In Charlotte, where there are six-hundred-plus churches, yet there weren't many doing outreach-focused ministry. Wonderful churches, but if you use the illustration of Paul being minister to the Gentiles and Peter being minister to the Jews (those with "orthodox" backgrounds), there were many "Peter" churches doing a wonderful job reaching those folks. But there weren't many reaching the five to six hundred thousand people of this city who weren't going to church. So as I studied, associated with Willow Creek and Saddleback, and prayed, I wrote a seventy-page position paper on where I wanted to go. I came back with much excitement, thinking that this is exactly what God wants. I called the leadership of the church together, about seventy leaders, on a retreat. I gave my presentation and said, "This is what I feel God wants us to do." And I mistakenly said (although I don't remember saying it, I was later told that I did), "If you all don't want to move with this, maybe I'm supposed to go somewhere else; I feel such passion for it." After eleven years some place, people love you and care for you, and nobody will object to you. So we came out of that weekend with a fresh new vision. I thought the leadership was on board. Until we had something very interesting happen. One of my associates died. Another one left to pursue a Ph.D. Another we had to fire. Another one took a call to another church. So I had four major people on staff leave, and I thought it was the Lord, because I said, "Well, these guys were recruited to a different kind of vision, and now we're moving a different direction." So I got approval by the session and recruited four new people who were totally committed to this new vision. Well, what happened over the next two years as the vision began to be lived out— worship changed, we became outreach-focused, I encouraged people to invite their lost friends to church—suddenly there was a malaise that began to slip into the church. Maybe even antipathy. People were feeling uncomfortable, like their church had been taken away: "David doesn't love me anymore." Charismatics: "My worship needs aren't getting met." Evangelicals: "We aren't preaching the Word." Mainline: "What is *this*?" So I had people in all three camps mad at me, though I didn't know it because they weren't talking to me. What I did realize was that what the leadership had given me back on that retreat was verbal assent. But in their hearts, they weren't really ready to go. They were questioning it. They loved me so much, after eleven years, that they nodded. But they didn't really get behind it, and they didn't tell me. Which probably says some things about my leadership, that they didn't feel able to come and talk to me.

**Chandler**: Why wouldn't they come and talk with you?

**Chadwick:** I think part of it was the success. We'd grown for eleven years. How do you question the growth? We'd gone from one hundred eighty people in a sleepy little church. The Presbytery told me it was going to close within five years. And it was suddenly hugely successful. So I think it was, "Who are we to question David? What do we know?" But some people began to talk, and some elders began to listen, and there was this undercurrent of resentment toward me, and the vision. So about two years in, I got this "feel" where I knew five hundred people were real excited about the vision; they were new and were really excited about their faith. You've got four hundred in the church who are really upset. About another seven hundred don't have a clue; they're kind of in that mushy middle. I've got an elder board with people chewing their ears all the time. My staff is totally behind me. So I've created a leadership division in the church. We had meetings, tough meetings; people were hurting. For about a year, we just had to halt the vision.

**Chandler:** What got you beyond the impasse?

**Chadwick:** Eventually I had to get up before the elder board, and later the congregation, and say to them, "There's a leadership schism here, and I'm partly to blame for it. I'm sorry, and we're going to work it out. Please forgive me."

**Chandler:** What were you sorry for?

**Chadwick:** I was sorry for being so aggressive and moving ahead before the leadership was really with me. In the end, Forest Hill's success came because we found unity at the leadership level. You've got to have that unity before moving forward. If you've got that, the church body can complain and gripe, and it doesn't matter. If you don't, it's going to be problematic. We didn't have that. We had verbal assent but not heart assent.

**Chandler:** So where, from there?

**Chadwick:** It was really hard. I kept going back to, "What has God called us to do? How can we be faithful to that vision?" Some would say, how audacious to think you're the only person in the church who gets vision. But where, in the Bible, does God give vision to a group of people? Number one, God gives vision to the leader. I'm not arrogant; people know that. But this is what I really think we're supposed to do. The bottom line is that we reached a kind of impasse. The elder board asked me to go on vacation and pray for a sense of where God wanted me to go. So I went away thinking, "Do I need to resign? Do I go to another place? What should I do?" And I read a little book by Henri Nouwen, *In the Name of Jesus,* which talks about leadership in the twenty-first century. The gist of the book is that leaders need to lay down their lives. The purpose of the leaders is to serve the sheep and not have the sheep serve them. The example is Jesus to Peter in John 21, "If you love me, feed my sheep." If you do that, then later in that chapter [Nouwen] says you may be "carried to a place where you don't want to go." Nouwen used that as a springboard to say that leaders are ones who learn to trust other people, who might be capable of taking them to a place where they don't want to go. It was a "light bulb" moment. I knew the Lord was speaking to me. I needed to be able to let go and let the Body lead me, perhaps to a place I didn't want to go. So I came back and at the first meeting—a tense one, as you can imagine—and I said, "Where do you all want to go?" It led to a new chapter in our church.

**Chandler:** What marked the first chapter?

**Chadwick:** Ninety percent of it was transfer growth.

**Chandler:** So the first chapter was personality driven, based on your ability to cement coalitions.

**Chadwick:** Yes.

**Chandler:** The second chapter of growth was vision-driven, but forceful and directive in such a way that it added one more volatile coalition to the mix, and resulted in high instability in the church.

**Chadwick:** That's right.

**Chandler:** And now a third chapter, based on a model of servant leadership, which allows God to speak to you, but to the people also.

**Chadwick:** It includes them in the process. Now I still believe God gives vision to his person, the leader. But there is a need for consensus among leadership before you move forward.

**Chandler:** What's this chapter been like?

**Chadwick:** It's been wonderful. We've been in it since the night when I asked leaders the question, "Where do you think we ought to go?" There was dead silence. Finally one of the key elders, well-respected, a big influencer, said, "Well, where do *you* think we ought to go?"

**Chandler:** As soon as you quit striving for the authority to make those decisions, it was granted to you.

**Chadwick:** Exactly. And I said, "I've got to be honest with you; I really believe that this is where God wants us to go." Over the course of the next year, three of the most vocal elders left, angrily. When one in particular left, the Sunday he was gone, it was as if a cloud lifted from this church.

**Chandler:** Do you believe that, in order to have unity, some people might have to leave?

**Chadwick:** Absolutely. This whole thing of "closing the back door" [keeping people from leaving the church]—certainly we want to do that with people who need ministry—but I think we need to leave it open for some.

**Chandler:** How can pastors or church leaders discern whether a back-door departure is a tragic fracture of fellowship, or when it is a necessary moving on for the body of Christ?

**Chadwick:** How much emotion is there, and what kind? Them, me, the congregation? With some, you might need to go and say, "I'm so sorry, let's be reconciled"…but it's still time to leave. With others, they don't want that. You shake the dust off your feet. You let one another go, and that's okay.

**Chandler**: What else have you had to let go of, as a leader, in order for it to continue to grow?

**Chadwick:** I had to let go of my need to be liked, for everybody to like me. I had to let go of finding my identity in my job. I had to let go of worrying about my reputation in the community. What I had to focus on was, "Is this what God is calling us to do?" I had to keep on answering yes to that question.

**Chandler**: How did you maintain focus on God's calling rather than finding your sufficiency in other peoples' opinions of you?

**Chadwick:** My wife continued to tell me that, no matter what, she loved me. Second, my remarkable staff—one or another would come into my office and say, "David, you need a brain dump?" Or, "You're okay. You're on the right track. Keep at it." It's real encouragement.

**Chandler**: What have you had to pick up in order to continue to grow?

**Chadwick:** It's so much easier to get already-convinced people to join your church. They already know how to pray. They've been to church, they read their Bibles, and they know how to give. It's so much harder to take new people and teach them all of those things, especially the "giving" part. The truth is that most new seeker-believers don't give much until one or two years into their involvement in the church. Rick Warren's right: the money *is* in the mouth of the fish. It just takes a long time to get it out! It's so much easier to get fish that are already cleaned. But when you have to catch them, scale them, dress them, get the meat off the bones, then it's hard work. Yet, there's nothing more exciting than seeing a new believer growing in the faith.

**Chandler**: As a leader, it's choose your poison: you either have to deal with already-churched people, who bring their presuppositions and expectations about how church ought to work; or you have to "catch and clean the new fish."

**Chadwick:** I went back and looked at every person who joined our church and then left. We lost about two hundred fifty people in the transition process. Every single person who left had joined here from another church. Not one person left who came here and accepted Christ here. Most of those who left transferred to another church.

**Chandler**: So you deal with the people leaving in a growing church by understanding that most of those who leave don't result in a net loss to the Kingdom.

**Chadwick:** It's just the fat shifting in the body of Christ! I think it's something like divorce. You get one divorce, and it's easier the second time. You leave one church to come here, it's easier to leave this church. When we get people from other churches, there's a swelling of pride in our hearts (I know there was in mine): "Joe Blow left First Whatever to come here because we're special." Truth is, it won't be long till Joe gets dissatisfied with you, and leaves you to go someplace else. Once he's experienced the trauma of leaving another church, it'll be easier for him to leave here, too.

**Chandler**: So just because a new couple comes into your church carrying a Bible and using offering envelopes, it doesn't mean that they don't need to be led too.

**Chadwick**: Exactly. I'd say many of those transfers come into the church expecting to build a relationship with you, the pastor. Then, a year in, when they find out you're not going to be close buddies, or there's a conflict about belief, or the church is going in a different direction, they're the first ones to turn around and leave. It's amazing to me how many deeply spiritual people seem to base it all on whether they have a personal relationship with the pastor.

**Chandler**: You have a gregarious personality, but in a church of thousands of people, you can't base your church's growth on your personal ability to have relationships with new people. How do you deal with that?

**Chadwick**: Oh man, I knew everybody's name, up till about one thousand. I'd spend every Monday calling every visitor. I'd introduce them to the congregation with a personal touch. But beyond one thousand, it just got so overwhelming. Sometimes I'd call them up to say "Hi," and they'd say, "Oh, by the way, pastor," and then just pour out deep personal problems for an hour. I was unwittingly setting up the expectation that I'd be their personal friend. Then they'd go to the hospital and I wouldn't come. And they'd say, "What's wrong, don't you love me? Where were you? I needed you." I was setting up an unrealistic expectation.

**Chandler**: What did you offer in lieu of a personal relationship?

**Chadwick**: I'd say in new members' classes, *"Don't* expect that I'll get to know you."

**Chandler**: A clear statement about boundaries and expectations.

**Chadwick**: Yes. And the elders backed me up. They said, "If the elders go to the hospital, David will come see us; but if you go to the hospital, we'll come see you. Don't expect to see the pastor." The joke was, "If David comes to see you in the hospital, this may be your last gasp!" The elders helped a lot.

**Chandler**: Obviously, you had a system of pastoral care in place, so that people who went to the hospital got visited…just not by you.

**Chadwick**: Our pastoral care people and home groups do it better than I would have done it.

**Chandler**: So the pastor can say, "I'm not going to visit," *if* the pastor has led in such a way that the whole body of Christ has learned to give mutual self-care.

**Chadwick**: One of the things I say around here is, "Which is easier: a few pastors caring for thousands of people, or let the whole body of Christ operate as the body?" That's a core value here.

**Chandler**: Where are you most "at home" as a leader?

**Chadwick**: Up front, casting vision. Seeing things that God wants that many people can't see. Getting people excited about that vision. When I got back from Israel—the church sent us there for our twentieth anniversary—I said, "You know, it's like coming out of halftime. I hope I'm here another twenty years. Here's where we are. Here's where we're going. This is where we need to be. These are the adjustments we need to make in the second half." Casting vision.

**Chandler**: What kind of adjustments does a minister entering the second half of ministry need to make to lead effectively?

**Chadwick**: I think the first question you need to ask is, "Am I going to make it? What's it going to take for me, for us, to finish strong?" With that as the goal, then what do I ease back on (like visiting the hospital), and what do I move forward with? For me, I had to quit counseling. I have a counseling degree. But I had to quit seeing people three and four times. It had to become "once and referral." I'd see people a few times, and they'd leave the church. Sometimes they'll do that when you know too much about them. They're so uncomfortable that you know they've had an abortion, or struggle with homosexuality. Now, with the referral, they get better counseling, plus, they can stay in the church. It's been a real blessing. So you ascertain what it's going to take to get there. Then you go to the leadership of the church, tell them what you need, get their input and consensus, and show them what's going to substitute for it. You show them how the changes are going to give the church equal or better value. How it's going to be better. Instead of one person visiting you in the hospital, it's going to be five, or a dozen. But you have to get the leadership on board.

**Chandler**: In many places in the South, if it's not the pastor visiting, it doesn't seem to count as a real visit.

**Chadwick**: You have to teach people to look at Scripture. I never see any model in the Bible where one person takes care of all the people. The illustration that the shepherd takes care of the sheep breaks down when you realize that the primary New Testament image of the church is not a shepherd-sheep relationship, but the image of the body of Christ. One person is never intended to care for sixty, six hundred, or six thousand in the church. It's not supposed to work like that. The biblical concept is of gifts, and the gifts of all people build up the body. As I understand it, the ones with gifts of mercy should be caring for people in the body.

**Chandler**: So moving away from a "shepherd-sheep" model to a "body of Christ" model not only enables the church to grow numerically, but also enables it to grow spiritually, because all people are employing their gifts in ministry, not just the staff.

**Chadwick**: I think a lot of people are using the "sheep-shepherd" picture of the church. And I just don't see it as the central New Testament model.

**Chandler**: If there is a shepherd in the New Testament, it's Christ—not the pastor.

**Chadwick**: Exactly. It's Jesus. He's the Shepherd. "The LORD is my shepherd, I shall not want" (Ps. 23:1).

**Chandler**: What area of leadership is still "pay the rent" for you? What are some things that you have to do, though you don't find any great joy in doing them?

**Chadwick**: Overseeing a certain degree of administration. I've got session meetings, performance reviews, writing up my own annual goals, moderating meetings.

**Chandler**: You've mentioned the "session" a couple of times. In what sense is remaining connected with a denomination important to you and your church?

**Chadwick**: It's relationship and accountability. We find great value in connectionalism. We're not out there on our own. We have brothers and sisters who can help us if we get off track. People will come to me offering help or asking, "Are you sure?" I find great comfort in that.

**Chandler**: So the "added value" of a denomination is support, fellowship, and accountability?

**Chadwick:** Yes.

**Chandler**: Many churches in the United States are on a plateau or are declining. Some have decades or even centuries of history and tradition and are very change-resistant. Many pastors and churches feel "stuck." Having led a church through many growth barriers, how would you counsel these church leaders as to how to begin to get unstuck?

**Chadwick**: I think the pastor first has to ask the question, "Do I want the church to grow?" And, as a part of that question, "Am I willing to pay the price for the changes that are coming if it grows?" Second, "Is the leadership on board with growth?" I think some people say they want to reach new people, but when you get right down to it, they don't want to deal with building campaigns and new people showing up. Here, we're starting to deal with nose-rings and green hair showing up. Are you willing to deal with it when people who are different show up? Those are the two key questions. Does the pastor want to grow? Does the leadership want to grow? Together, they can do it. There are huge prices. But if they stay together, no matter what the aches and pains in the body might be, if they really want it to happen, it can happen. You have to be willing to have your ears chewed on.

**Chandler**: So if the pastor's ready to grow, the first thing the pastor should do is confirm that church leaders are on board.

**Chadwick**: Come to a unified leadership consensus about growth. Then be prepared to weather the coming storms together.

**Chandler**: It's about unity?

**Chadwick**: Truth is, the pastor shouldn't unite the church; the music shouldn't unite the church. ("That's a contemporary music church, that's a traditional music church.") What has to unite the church is vision. If the vision is set, then how you get to that vision will define what you do at every other level: groups, pastoral care, worship, music, etc. Once vision is in place, methodology follows. Vision unites the church. If it doesn't, my guess is that this church splits. What happened here is that fringes of each one of the constituencies left (evangelicals, charismatics, mainlines). But the ones who stayed, even though they are different, united around the vision. They said, "We came here looking for 'this,' but you gave us *this,* and peoples' souls are being saved, and we're excited about that!" The vision keeps them together. It's about people coming into the Kingdom and having their lives transformed.

**Chandler**: I get the sense that you're using the word *vision* as synonymous with *evangelism.*

**Chadwick**: Well, for us, it is. That is our vision. It's our highest priority. I believe that if we really believe that Jesus came to seek and save the lost, then worship and fellowship and teaching and other things are secondary. They're important, but they're secondary. You've heard it said that there will be worship and fellowship in heaven. The only thing we won't do in heaven is reach lost people for Jesus Christ. So we've got to do that now. It's all either "so that" or "so what?" Everything we do in this church, we do "so that" we can reach people for Christ.

### Reflecting on the Trip: Questions for Continuing the Conversation

1. How does vision unite in ways that personality cannot?
2. In what ways can the possibility of a call to another venue for ministry disrupt, sharpen, or clarify leadership in your current setting? How can one maintain integrity and quality of leadership when the setting for the next chapter of ministry is uncertain?
3. At about eleven years, David and the congregation reached an impasse. While long tenure is widely praised as necessary for effective ministry, what traps does it also bring? How can pastor and congregation anticipate and negotiate issues exacerbated due to long tenure?
4. What do you learn from David about how to measure and evaluate the significance of people departing the congregation? When are individual departures positive for the congregation's future? What are the tools by which leaders can accurately read the message given in a departure?
5. David had a sense of his ministry at "half time." How can pastors and other congregational leaders identify where they are "in the game" and minister strategically out of that assessment?

5

*Interview with* **Brian McLaren**
Cedar Ridge Community Church, Spencerville, Maryland
www.crcc.org or www.brianmclaren.net

# Courageous Intelligence

Brian McLaren is author of *A Generous Orthodoxy,*[1] *The Church on the Other Side,*[2] *Finding Faith,*[3] and many other books. A former professor of English at the University of Maryland, Brian was pastor of Cedar Ridge Community Church in Spencerville, Maryland, at the time of our conversation. He is a leading voice in North American conversations about the emerging church.

### Here's a Trip-tik™ of things to watch for:

✓ McLaren's focus on urban and suburban people not reached by existing churches, including an acute understanding of the intellectual and cultural barriers preventing conversations between these people and congregations
✓ Factors leading to the decision to "reboot" the congregation, and the processes and outcomes of this major leadership move
✓ Struggles caused by the church changing sizes, and by incorporating people with little or no Christian "baseline"

---

[1]Brian McLaren, *A Generous Orthodoxy: Why I Am a Missional, Evangelical, Post/Protestant, Liberal/Conservative, Mystical/Poetic, Biblical, Charismatic/Contemplative, Fundamentalist/Calvinist, Anabaptist/Anglican, Methodist, Catholic, Green, Incarnational, Depressed-yet-Hopeful, Emergent, Unfinished CHRISTIAN* (Grand Rapids: Zondervan, 2004).
[2]Brian McLaren, *The Church on the Other Side* (Grand Rapids: Zondervan, 2003).
[3]Brian McLaren, *Finding Faith: A Self-Discovery Guide for Your Spiritual Quest* (Grand Rapids: Zondervan, 2000).

✓ The dance between "control" and "influence" in leadership, and the evolution of leadership styles as the fledgling church emerges
✓ The bias toward radical rather than incremental change
✓ Transparent humanity and confessional humility in a leader
✓ Hope-based, rather than fear-based, theology and leadership

---

**Chandler**: Tell me about the decisive spiritual event that led to your vision for starting Cedar Ridge Community Church.

**McLaren**: We had started a home Bible study for college students, graduate students, and a couple of faculty members at the University of Maryland. It grew up to about forty people. We realized that there were very few, if any, churches in the area that we could bring these people to. The cultural and intellectual barriers would have been too great. So in some ways, it was just a decision to try to take care of these people who had become Christians.

**Chandler**: By "cultural and intellectual barriers," you're referring to...

**McLaren**: Some of it is as superficial as clothing style. None of these people would have owned a suit. And some of it was as profound as the relationship between faith and science. Many of these were graduate students and intellectually alive people. So if they were to walk into a place where they had to believe the earth was 6,000 years old or something like that, it just wouldn't work. Political issues, too. If every time they walked into the door of a church the expectation was that they were conservative Republicans, that would have been a problem, too. These people came from all over the map.

**Chandler**: So the typical church culture as an anti-intellectual, conservative, Republican, button-down community was a barrier to reaching this group of people, for reasons that were not spiritual.

**McLaren**: Exactly right. As an example, one couple in the church invited me over one night to their house, to a party for a bunch of their neighbors. They didn't tell anybody who I was; I was just a friend to these neighbors. I was sitting on the couch, talking to this lady, and she asked me how I knew this couple. I said, "We go to the same church," very carefully avoiding saying that I was a pastor so that I didn't ruin a good conversation.

**Chandler**: Kiss of death?

**McLaren**: Right! And when I said, "I go to their church," she said, "I wish I could go to church. I would *love* it if I could go to church." I said, "Well what's keeping you away?" She said, "I'm pro-choice, and you can only go to church if you're pro-life." So the message she got was, "Unless you already agree with us on a whole list of social, cultural, and theological issues, you are not welcome among us." We ironically convey that we are a nonwelcoming community. So, in some ways, the urge for starting a church was the urge to create a community that was rooted in Scripture and has a deep belief in Christ, but that is also welcoming to people wherever they are coming from.

**Chandler**: How did you get this vision off of ground zero? How did you attract the critical mass of people to form a cohesive community?

**McLaren**: Honestly, I think we failed. One of my mottos in life is, "Anything worth doing is worth doing twice." What happened between 1982 and 1987 is that we realized that we had created a community that had become increasingly less welcoming. The more we developed our own little Christian subculture, the less welcoming we were. We *wanted* to be accepting of other people; but we created our own set of barriers. Some of it was even the relational closeness of the group. We were very close as a group. We were in each other's homes all the time. Ironically, that crowded out the chance to have non-Christian friends. I would say that because of the closeness of that fellowship, we all lost most of our non-Christian friends.

**Chandler**: A church conceptually founded on inclusion found that its own organizational life created structures of exclusion.

**McLaren**: Exactly. Exactly right. I become extremely frustrated about this in 1987. I had left my job as a college English teacher in 1986. Within about a year, I felt that I might have made a mistake, because I didn't want to get stuck in this little religious ghetto. Although everyone was very happy and loved each other, I was somewhat claustrophobic. Partly, I think, because the Holy Spirit gave me a gift of evangelism, I wasn't happy just tending the flock. So I went to our elders, our leadership team, in 1987, and said, "I have the most to lose with this, because I've quit my job and am working for the church now." I also said, "Why don't we shut down the church, and for about ten months go into a prenatal stage to start a new church next year?" It was kind of a radical proposal. But our leadership team said "yes." We decided to move into a new location…"We'll choose a new name; we'll choose a new philosophy of ministry; we'll rewrite all of our documents about our mission statement, vision statement, statement of beliefs; we'll start all over again." And we'd invite all of the one hundred or so people who were part of the church at that time to be the church-planting team for a new church in about a year.

**Chandler**: So you all had, in a sense, a grace-filled death, and a resurrection.

**McLaren**: Yes. I remember thinking (though I haven't told many people this), "Maybe I'll just leave. The church is so happy as it is; I don't want to mess it up." But the church was still young enough that if I had left, I don't think it would have gone on. So then I was left with the option of, "Do I leave and let it die on its own?" This seemed like the most compassionate option, because I wasn't willing to stay and be stuck in the status quo. The first phase of that went really well, because about eighty of those one hundred adults went with us.

**Chandler***:* The other twenty left, went to other churches, dropped out?

**McLaren**: I would say they went to other churches. Part of the issue was that we moved. The new location was just too far for some people.

**Chandler**: Do you find that it's often true that when there is a re-envisioning of the church's mission, the people who leave land in other churches and are not lost to the Kingdom?

**McLaren**: Oh, that's very true. Our real challenge was not that, but came later. Because between 1988 and 1990, the group went from eighty to over two hundred adults, and went through all the traumas of getting over that "200 barrier" that people talk about. We also had this trauma: the new people who came in really were unchurched. So the new start really worked. Then, the eighty Christians who made the change with us were faced with a problem: the new people who came in weren't "just like us." The church was never going to be like it used to be. So from 1990 to 1994, we had a lot of trauma, as one person after another from that original core group left the church. These were good friends. We loved each other. Every single leaving was a tremendous personal loss.

**Chandler**: The most painful personal time in your pastoral career?

**McLaren**: I would say I made it through that time on sort of will and determination and a little bit of a fighting spirit. But at the end of that time, I was exhausted. I would say that led to 1994 to 1996, which were really the toughest times.

**Chandler**: So the church had difficulty adjusting both to the whole ethos of unchurched people, and also the "feel" of the church having so many more people there?

**McLaren**: Exactly. I didn't have the language for this at the time, but I think the other, deeper, issue that was going on at the time was that the newer people who were coming in were postmodern. And when they became Christians, they were never going to become modern-style Christians. I think that was a big surprise to this original group. I think they thought, "These people will become Christians and they'll be just like us." They became Christians, but not just like the others. That was a tough go.

**Chandler**: Can you state concisely what you learned about what it means to be a "postmodern Christian" as opposed to an older-style "modern Christian"?

**McLaren**: I don't think anybody knows what a "postmodern Christian" is yet. I think we're still in the process of trying to figure that out. I've written a book on it called *A New Kind of Christian*.[4]

**Chandler**: Since we don't know what a postmodern Christian is yet, were there any thinkers, teachers, or models that helped you grow through this? You obviously made it through that famous "200 barrier."

---

[4]Brian McLaren, *A New Kind of Christian: A Tale of Two Friends on a Spiritual Journey* (San Francisco: Jossey Bass Books, 2001).

**McLaren**: The church growth movement helped me in the 1980s. So Rick Warren, Bill Hybels, and John Maxwell were a huge help to me. I think a lot of us, by the 1990s, were having second thoughts about the church growth movement, saying that it was helping us in some ways but not in others. In 1994, when I was so tired after these four years of increased conflict, I was really ready to do some rethinking. I felt something wasn't working. I felt, in some ways, my practice was way ahead of my theory, and I needed my theory to catch up. I remember at that point I stumbled across—I have no idea how I found it—a book by Walsh and Middleton called *Truth Is Stranger Than It Used To Be*.[5] They talk about this shift from a modern to a postmodern world, and the effect that has on the Bible and the gospel. I remember, when I read that book, it started clicking with a lot I stuff I had read and thought way back in graduate school. That had a big influence on me.

**Chandler**: You sensed something intuitively, perhaps out of your background as an English professor, and it led to a decisive philosophy of leadership or evangelism.

**McLaren**: When you start to consider the possibility that there's a whole new culture emerging; that the dominant way of doing things is related to a dominant philosophy, and that there's an emerging philosophy that will yield an emerging new way of doing things…in some ways we often think of this related to the economy. We talk about the "Old Economy" and "New Economy." We are aware that the rules change in the new economy. So you're right: there are new forms of leadership, new approaches to evangelism; I think there will be new ways that we approach theology and the church.

**Chandler**: Can you give an example of how you had to "rebalance your leadership portfolio" given these emerging changes?

**McLaren**: I was very lucky in this regard, John, because I don't think I was very good at the top-down, C.E.O. style of leadership. In some ways, feeling the freedom to let go of that was a bit like David taking off Saul's armor. I think it was a little more true to who I was. Part of that is related to my own development—I think at the age of thirty-seven or thirty-eight I realized, "I am not a good boss." I work with volunteers extremely well. But to be a good boss of paid employees is almost the opposite.

**Chandler**: So much for supervision, evaluation, and all of that…

**McLaren**: Exactly. And because I have a very strong pastoral bond with people, if I would give them an evaluation as a boss, we would almost cry [*laughing*]. You know, I'd hurt their feelings and make them feel rejected as a human being, which I had no intention of doing. So I think I had permission, and my leaders gave me permission, to say, "I'm not a good

---

[5]J. Richard Middleton and Brian J. Walsh, *Truth Is Stranger Than It Used To Be: Biblical Faith in a Postmodern Age* (Downers Grove, Ill.: InterVarsity Press, 1995).

boss. We'll find other ways to make this thing work." So gradually we migrated to working as a team. We moved away from me being the "alpha male," and a hierarchical structure, to me being the leader of a group that functions as a team.

**Chandler**: How can you lead a church without being the alpha male? How can you move to a team-structure of leadership in churches that are primarily and historically governed congregationally? Or can you?

**McLaren**: I wouldn't say this is a matter of right and wrong. The analogy that comes to my mind is parenting. When you have very small children, you aren't in the "command and control" mode. You can't tell babies what to do; it doesn't matter. You just have to help them get through that time. Then you have a period where you *can* tell them what to do, with more or less success. Then comes the strange time when they stop wanting to do what you tell them to do. And then you move from control to influence. As parents, we move from control to influence. I think the same thing is true of leaders. We move out of the control phase. Part of having a maturing church is having people who don't want to be told what to do anymore. Because we've succeeded at helping them mature, they now need to be treated with more respect. We all know the verse that says, "Honor your father and mother." Yet Ephesians 6 says, "Parents, don't frustrate your children." I think it's saying parents have to honor their children. As leaders, we should learn how to honor the people we've led. It's a change in the way we see them.

**Chandler***:* You're the father of four teenagers, so you had to figure out when to let go of command and control with them. At what point did you begin to move to that model in your church leadership?

**McLaren**: First, I was never really good at command and control. But I think, honestly, as a church planter, you end up with a lot more authority than the average pastor coming into the existing church. I remember, mid-1990s, feeling that I had way too much power, more than was good for me or good for the church. I remember breakfast with a fellow I had led to Christ. He said, "Brian, you are right 85 percent of the time, which is higher than anybody else I know. But it's the other 15 percent that makes you dangerous." I thought that this was a very wise statement. He was trying to say to me, "You have to be listening to other people." The fact that you're right so much so much of the time means that people may follow you when they shouldn't.

**Chandler**: The most dangerous leaders are the ones with the most credibility.

**McLaren**: Yes. So I started going out of the way in a meeting to tell people that I wasn't going to state my opinion. I wanted to hear everyone else's opinion.

**Chandler**: So you moved to a team-based form of church leadership because that was spiritually healthy for you and the congregation?

**McLaren**: Yes. There was an odd time—and I wouldn't recommend this for everybody—when I didn't attend staff meetings. While I'm not a particularly domineering person, I was the planter. So it was good for me to stay away and let the staff wrestle with issues. I remember one of my elders said something at this time that was so hard for me. It took a lot of courage for him to say it to me. He said, "Brian, stop bringing us solutions and start bringing us problems." When I would think through the problem and come up with a solution, it squelched them. They just became rubber-stamps. He said, "You might have a solution in your mind; just don't tell us." He was, in a way, pleading with me to show them more honor, to give them more ownership to feel the problem and not just rubber-stamp my solution.

**Chandler**: Part of good leadership is not to come to premature closure and cut off the full richness of what might happen when the fuller body of Christ interacts with a situation.

**McLaren**: Exactly right. Then again, I am so results-oriented that I just want a decision. What they were telling me was, "The process is really important." Those were hard lessons for me. I spent 3–4 years getting it 20 percent of the time and not getting it 80 percent. And now maybe I'm at the point where I get it 80 percent of the time and still don't get it 20 percent.

**Chandler**: You said you were "results-oriented." How have you learned to back off from results and pay attention to process in your leadership?

**McLaren**: One of the questions I ask myself is, "Why am I in such a hurry?" There is this strange feeling—it's as if we're trying to get something finished. Maybe it's an American phenomenon. Then I realize, "This thing is never going to be finished." A church never gets finished. One of our elders, one of the guys who had to have the courage to stand up and get in my face—he said there's a stretch of road he drives from an airport to an office in a certain city. He flies into that airport, rents a car, and makes that two-hour drive to the office. He's been doing it every couple of months for ten years. He said when he first started the drive, they were doing road construction on the first couple of miles. Through the years, they continued going down the whole stretch of road. He said the last time he flew into the city, they were rebuilding the first part of the road again. Then it struck him: "Roads are never finished." I think that's true of churches. A realization I've had is that I've got to stop rushing. My rushing will make things worse. I can see it in a lot of other people better than I can see it in myself. I've been very involved in missions; I was the chairman of the board of a mission agency. And foreign missions—all the talk about, "We'll reach the world by such-and-such a date"—has made us do some things that are really harmful, in the long run, to the cause of Christ. So I started seeing that I had some desire or need to finish a job that doesn't get finished. When I let go of that, I started to enjoy the journey more.

**Chandler**: "Haste" exhibits a lack of trust in God and superimposes a human agenda onto a Kingdom agenda that may not have a timetable, such as the end of the fiscal year, end of the millennium, or anything like that.

**McLaren**: What makes it worse is that we assume God is as paranoid and neurotic as we are to get the job done. I remember Phil Yancey's book saying, "Of all the people in the world, Jesus is the one person who seemed not to have a messiah complex." Jesus didn't say, "We're going to reach the world by the end of the first century." He didn't use those kinds of tense deadlines. He used images of seed planted in a field, images of gradual growth. The seasons. I think that's healthier.

**Chandler**: So relaxing from your "hurry sickness" was a factor in your leadership being more effective and your church growing. What other things helped you all get through the "stuck" times and grow through new barriers?

**McLaren**: Well, we certainly aren't a megachurch. We average from 700–900 people on a Sunday.

**Chandler**: What gave you the momentum to get there?

**McLaren**: You know, I think momentum comes and goes. To be honest, I was in a conversation recently with staff about being unhappy with the level of momentum we have now. In our church, we had some persistent problems in the mid-1990s, and when we solved them, we had the momentum to grow. One was that we didn't have a building. We didn't have a building because we didn't know how to deal with money. We didn't know how to deal with money because the numbers we were looking at were way beyond anything we had experience with. So it took us awhile to get comfortable with what you had to deal with to buy land and all the rest. We also had to get comfortable as a church with growing up and talking about money in mature ways. Like a lot of seeker-oriented churches, we had minimized money. We didn't want people to think that we just wanted them to come for their money. So we downplayed that subject. One of the best things that happened to our church is when we had to raise money to buy land. Because we had to say to the church, this is *your* church, and if you want to get to the next step, you have to make sacrifices.

**Chandler**: Was that an area of personal growth for you as well?

**McLaren**: It was an area of huge personal growth for me to ask other people to make sacrifices. Like many church planters, I was ready to make huge sacrifices myself. It was hard to ask them to make sacrifices. But you know what? It's a lot like children again. You don't want to ask your little children to make sacrifices. But you know that when they get older, adulthood is about sacrifice. So it was about me realizing that the church was growing up. I needed to pay it that respect. By excluding the church from sacrifice, I was keeping the church immature. I'll never forget the day we had done a big fund-raising campaign. We had hoped to raise $900,000; that was our highest goal. We expected $600,000 and hoped for $900,000.

And when we tallied up the gifts and they came to $1,400,000, I was just speechless and in tears. I realized, "These people care about this mission." It was a wonderful day. In our story, that was a major part of momentum.

**Chandler:** Many pastors talk about how a bricks-and-mortar issue—a building, a financial campaign, or a relocation—triggered spiritual maturing in their congregations. That sounds to be the case with your church.

**McLaren:** Yes, and it's interesting: now that we've solved that problem and gotten over that hump (we moved into our building eighteen months ago), I'm saying, "What's the next challenge?" We certainly don't want to get complacent now. We live twenty minutes from inner-city Baltimore, inner-city D.C. I'm saying, "Now that we've got the walls up, how do we live outside the walls?" We have to look outside. How can we make a difference in our neighborhoods, our communities, and the areas of great needs around us? It is very exciting to think about that next stage of mission and vision.

**Chandler:** Some churches see a church planting movement, others see a hands-on mission movement. What else can churches do to thrive after they've built the building of their dreams?

**McLaren:** In my book *The Church on the Other Side,* I use a term "program." By "program," I mean a combination of activities we put together in a given year. A lot of fads come down the road: "Here's the latest program!" We try to imitate it. It helps a few churches, but it doesn't help a lot of churches. I think the reason is that  every church is unique. The challenge for church leaders is creatively to listen, to talk, and to figure out that answer in their unique situation. There are internal factors: "Where are we weak as a community? Where do we need to grow in Christ-likeness?" There are also external factors: "What are the needs of our community? How is the culture changing?" So it's hard for me to think of specifics there. I think each situation is so unique.

**Chandler:** It pertains to each church's particular calling from God.

**McLaren:** Right.

**Chandler:** Given that the answer is always contextual, do you have some general words of hope for pastors and churches are who are "stuck?" Maybe they're stuck at a growth barrier, like the 200 barrier. Or maybe they're stuck in terms of not figuring out what it will take to reach the kind of person who would never come to the church because of the church's culture. Or maybe they are stuck in their own spiritual walk.

**McLaren:** Getting unstuck is a tough challenge. If I were to offer a piece of hope, it would be this: I think there is more hope in radical change than in incremental change. If the church is really stuck, and keeps trying small measures to bring about change, usually those small measures are at best tolerated and at worst fought. We fight so many battles over small things. "Can we get a guitar, or overhead projector, drums, PowerPoint?"

**Chandler:** Every small battle exacts a pound of flesh.

**McLaren**: Yes, and everyone gets tired and demoralized. When you lose those small battles, your most visionary people leave your church. They say, "If this church can't solve small problems like this, why even try?" Well, that leaves you with congregations with very loyal but change-averse people. So if a church knows that it is stuck and needs change, it would be smarter for it to engineer its own crisis. Engineer radical change. I call it "maximizing discontinuity." I'll give an example. For us, as I started getting the idea that we're in an emerging postmodern culture, an age of radical transition, I hoped at first to lead the church in the right direction without ever telling them what I was thinking. I hoped to be subtle and gradual about it. That didn't work. Eventually, I had some very open conversations with my elders about it. I put some of my thoughts in writing, which became my first book. I found that when I was very direct with them about what I was thinking, they were very receptive. I think a lot of pastors can go to their church leaders and say, "Let me tell you what I'm thinking." Not, "Let me tell you what we're going to do," but, "I'm having fears about this...I'm discouraged about this...hopeful about this." Just start talking and let it be a conversation, so the lay leaders don't feel that something is being foisted upon them and they're being forced into something. Leaders see what kind of questions you're asking and what changes you're going through. They're brought in on the conversation. Then you get to a point where if they start to "catch" it through a process, then they'll be willing to help you do a revolution.

**Chandler**: So in the emerging postmodern culture, people will not respond to being nickeled-and-dimed to death over small changes, but will, in a process, give their hearts to revolutionary change?

**McLaren**: Not always. One of the challenges for a leader is that if you're going to try to be a leader in this, you're going to have to be willing to lose. That's only fair. If we're not willing to lose, we're working under a "control" model, not an "influence" model. When you're influencing, people can say no. But I think you're right. I just read a business article about the new economy that said, "Bigger isn't better and smaller isn't better; *faster* is better." Doesn't matter whether you're big or small. If you can evolve faster, you're in a better position in the new economy. I thought to myself, what trouble we'd be in if that's true in churches. To me, the biggest change churches need to make is not in worship style, music style, preaching style, or anything like that. It's in their attitude toward change itself. If I, as a pastor, could make one change in a congregation, I would try to preach, lead, discuss, pray, and do everything I could to help that congregation change its attitude toward change. This goes to some very deep issues. When do we believe, as a church, the best days are? Are the best days behind us, or ahead of us? If we believe the best days are ahead of us, then we are possessed with a vision that makes us want to align with what those better days in the future are about. I think this brings up some fascinating theological insights. For instance, how does eschatology work? Rather than our eschatology telling us that the world's about to end tomorrow, so we better have a last-minute burst of activity, we say, "No, whether or not the world ends tomorrow, God wants us to have a vision of hope for the future." That then makes us say, "Why waste my time?"

**Chandler**: "The kingdom of God is at hand" (Mk. 1:15, KJV); can you join God in what God is doing?

**McLaren**: Exactly right. There's a very hopeful future. If we as church leaders can change our attitudes toward change and have a hopeful view of the future, I think this is a real leverage point. It involves a very big rhetorical change. (I know I sound like an old English teacher!) One of the big buttons to push in rhetoric is the button of fear. "Terrible things are ahead; we'd better get our act together!" Or calling people back to the old ways: "The present is bad and the future will be worse." Well, that's like motivating by guilt. It might work for a while, but in the long run, you paint yourself into a corner. It's an act of self-sabotage. In the long run, the motivation is always hope. God is going to win; the gospel is all about hope.

### Reflecting on the Trip: Questions for Continuing the Conversation

1. Missiologists speak of the problem of "redemption and lift," the process of how new Christians are, upon salvation and introduction into ongoing congregational life, distanced from connection to the culture from which they were redeemed. How can leaders help churches avoid an insular disconnectedness from the communities of which they are a part, and which they are (presumably) trying to reach?

2. How do pastors "honor the people they lead" and accept congregational leaders as part of a leadership team, without abdicating their key leadership role?

3. Brian uses an analogy of parenting children through developmental stages as a metaphor for leading a church. What other organic analogies come to mind that offer insight into a leadership style that evolves in living relationships?

4. How can church leaders and pastors move from "offering solutions" to "offering problems"? To what extent is maturing leadership a move from giving answers to raising questions?

5. Basketball coach John Wooden used to teach, "Be quick but don't hurry." How can North American leaders learn to maintain "urgency" as a core value without devolving into a frenetic and harmful mode of leading?

6. Pastors are often called to lead churches to "put up walls" (buildings). How can leaders lead so that congregations simultaneously "move outside of walls" (mission)? How can building projects or relocations be tied to the congregation's calling to reach those outside of the building?

7. Whereas Bob Russell advocated steady incremental change strategies, Brian McLaren seems to favor more radical change strategies ("maximizing discontinuity"). How does one read context accurately to diagnose when one strategy is preferred over the other?
8. How can leaders help congregations grow in their attitudes toward change itself?

## 6

*Interview with* **Michael Slaughter**
Ginghamsburg, A United Methodist Church, Tipp City, Ohio
www.ginghamsburg.org

# Courageous Awakening

Located in a field sixteen miles north of Dayton, Ginghamsburg has an average weekly worship attendance of nearly four thousand in a town (Tipp City, Ohio) with a population of about six thousand. Not only does this church have incredible impact within a small community, it is also a torchbearer within its mainline denomination (United Methodist). Arriving in 1979, Michael Slaughter has awakened a sleepy church in a sleepy town to reach thousands of formerly unchurched people through an edgy, creative regional congregation. They are quite active in national and world mission causes.

**Here's a Trip-tik™ of things to watch for:**
✓ The philosophy that a church has to "get smaller" before it "gets bigger"
✓ The reframe from church members as "consumer/customers" to "missionaries"
✓ How Slaughter identifies and empowers "Joshuas and Deborahs" to become a new and vibrant leadership community alongside of an existing stagnant congregational leadership community
✓ How community impact and transformation measure a church's effectiveness, not congregational size
✓ The image of ministry as "sweet spot"

✓ How one moves from being "the pastor" to "empowering the pastors"
✓ Unapologetic statements of the primacy of Slaughter's family in relation to his role within the church

---

**Chandler:** Can you tell me a little bit about the Ginghamsburg story, and in particular about some of the vision you brought to this church when you came?

**Slaughter:** Ginghamsburg was like the typical little Methodist church. It was founded in 1863, really a by-product of the second Great Awakening, where the Methodists and Baptists spread all around the country and were essentially centered in the layperson—the Baptists in the lay farmer and the Methodist the lay leader, the circuit rider. The circuit riders established this church, preaching in this area in 1863, and there were fourteen conversions. Those fourteen conversions committed to form a class, a small group or cell, for mutual encouragement. By the 1870s they decided that if they were really going to be faithful to the Great Commission, to be the body of Christ and to reach out to the world, then they needed to raise money and build a little church. The church I came to, the little two-room country church, had outhouses until just eight years before I came. I came in 1979 and moved into the little two-room country church building down the road. It was built in 1876.

I was their first full-time pastor. Until the 1920s, it had been on a four-point circuit, and that circuit rider would preach, part-time. From the 1920s it was always served by a student from United Seminary, right here in Dayton, Ohio. When I came in 1979, I was the first full-time pastor. We had an annual budget of $27,000, ninety people, and I. In my twenty-seven-year-old naiveté, I was determined my life had to be given to true Kingdom work. That's winning the lost and setting the oppressed free. I believed that everyone who named the name of Jesus was a minister. I was not going to be a chaplain, to come and serve and take care of the church. I was going to equip the church for the sake of ministry. That's all I knew.

I had been in Campus Crusade for Christ in college, and the whole idea was the multiplication of cells. I came out of a kind of a very "First Church of Frigidaire" United Methodist upbringing where I didn't have any kind of relationship with Jesus. But I had a really transforming experience at the University of Cincinnati as a college student. At Campus Crusade for Christ, I discovered that we were here to make disciples. That became my ministry paradigm.

Our church quickly decreased from ninety to sixty. I think that anyone who understands the revolutionary movement of Christianity knows that you've got to get smaller before you get bigger. I think that's a constant. In the two decades plus I've been at Ginghamsburg, we're constantly losing people. Every week, I get a "Dear Pastor Pigface" letter. It's, "We don't like the music," or, "We know you're doing this for the young people, but who do you think pays the bills?" and, "We just think that what you're doing is out of the pit of hell. In Jesus' Love, signed…"

It's painful. My wife, at my son's baseball game last night, said to me, "Did you know that so-and-so is leaving? Man, this subtle, constant leaving is painful through all these years." There's this sense that the servant of God believes that we experience God in community but there is a complete loneliness that comes from both knowing the power of resurrection and the fellowship of suffering. Jesus was rejected; there's always a part of that. It creates a God-dependence all along.

The church in 1979 had ninety people. In 1994, when we moved to this campus, we had about twelve hundred people in worship per weekend. Now we have, including children who are not in adult worship celebrations, about 3,900 people a weekend.

**Chandler:** So even though the church decreased from ninety to sixty, something happened between 1979 and 1994 where other folk got on board with the same Kingdom vision that you brought?

**Slaughter:** Well, it's like I said: you get bigger by getting smaller. When I came to this church, I knew I couldn't minister to ninety people. Ninety was a bigger church than I could handle. That's why 70 percent of the churches are under one hundred in attendance: because one pastor can give them institutional care—hospital visits, home visits—and sacramental care—communion, baptism, weddings, and funerals. One pastor cannot give institutional care for more than ninety people.

However, one pastor can help empower ninety people to be a demonstration of *koinonia,* the radical, unconditional love of God. You know, you can organize people for a Disney boycott…but you cannot demonstrate the relentless-refusal-to-let-go-of-the-love-of-God to the world [doing that]. We're not going to change the world through boycotts. That's what Methodists do constantly. It's easy to become issue centered. That is why the apostle Paul said, "For I decided to know nothing among you except Jesus Christ, and him crucified" (1 Cor. 2:2). So that's me here, you know? I'm not going to be Republican or Democrat. People say, "Mike, preach on homosexuality this weekend." Nope. "I chose to know nothing while I was among you but Jesus Christ, and Christ crucified."

In the first three months while I was preaching, I began to look for people whose hearts were strangely warmed. And I began to talk about the radical nature of being a follower of Jesus and God's intentions for the community of Christ, preaching out of the book of Acts. What is this community supposed to be, what does it mean to be the hands and feet of

Jesus in the world, what does it mean to have a missionary mindset versus a consumer/customer? Our members get confused on that. They think they are the consumer/customer versus the missionary. You can spot those people out in the congregation who are getting it and hearing the voice of God. You see them taking notes. So I went to about nine or ten people and I said, "Carolyn and I are going to start a group in our home on Wednesday nights." This was going to be revolutionary because the godfathers and mothers of this church didn't want the church to be changed.

**Chandler:** Were they the ones who left in going from ninety to sixty?

**Slaughter:** Some of them left, some of them died, some of them went to the old folks home, and some of them are still here.

**Chandler:** How have they held on? How have you all coexisted?

**Slaughter:** Well, some of them get it! Yes, some of them; not everyone. Age is not chronological, it's a matter of spirit. There are some eighty-year-old people that are singing a new song. And there are some twenty-year-old people who are dried up, dead. Youth is eternity of the spirit.

What I did was to begin to meet with these people in my home while the godfathers and mothers wanted to continue to control the church and play church games: Christmas and missionary bazaars, chicken noodle dinners, and all that kind of stuff. What I did was teach this group of nine or ten people. We began to read Dietrich Bonhoeffer's *The Cost of Discipleship*[1] and George Hunter's *The Contagious Congregation.*[2] We asked, "What does it mean to be the revolutionary community of Jesus in our community and in the world? What does it mean if we, just this handful of ten people here, decided to live this thing sincerely and get involved with the poor in our community and really begin to be the hands of Jesus? So, ten of us began to practice being the hands and feet of Jesus…Those ten and I, as pastor, needed to finance this revolution. Therefore, of those ten I was discipling, I made one of them chair of the finance committee. I didn't try to change the mind or heart of the old chair. Too many of us were waiting for the chair to change. For resurrection to happen, death has to happen, either spiritually or physically. I needed to stay in the church so I made another one of them chair of the staff-parish committee. They became my Joshuas and Deborahs, the leaders of the revolution. Some of them are now staff in this church.

I created a new church within the old church and let the old people keep their little club. Instead of trying to change the old, I created a new event. So I have continued to focus on the pure DNA of the spirit of God with a few people to keep that intensity. And as I continue to focus, fanning

---

[1]Dietrich Bonhoeffer, *The Cost of Discipleship* (New York: Touchstone, 1959).

[2]George G. Hunter III, *The Contagious Congregation: Frontiers in Evangelism and Church Growth* (Nashville: Abingdon Press, 1979).

that to a fever, bringing it up to the boiling point in a few people, they infect others who infect others.

**Chandler:** And it's a self-replicating structure.

**Slaughter:** If you get into saying, "We're trying to build a church," it's going to be nothing but ashes. Don't go off and replicate Ginghamsburg Church. Coming here, I want this to be an icon, or a mirror, for you to look closely again at the vision God's already placed in you so that you could be faithful to that vision. It takes risk to do what you see here. You've got to follow the way of the cross. We're going to be crucified every week of our life if we're going where Jesus is going. So this has been painful.

**Chandler:** When did you come closest to falling during your leadership?

**Slaughter:** It's the times I wanted to quit, which happens. Sometimes you just feel beat up. When you're a little church, you just keep meeting so much resistance. It's hard on your family. I was making $12,000 a year. Other men and women my age, at that time, were making $30,000 a year in comparable professional fields with masters' degrees. In the early years especially, there's the temptation to be good so you can go to the bigger church.

**Chandler:** Climb the ladder.

**Slaughter:** Yeah, so I can go to "First Church." I never went to First Church. I'm still at the "little" Ginghamsburg you saw down the road. Of forty thousand United Methodist churches in the country, this one is in the top ten in size. That's the miracle of loaves and fishes.

"Ladder" is not a metaphor for the Kingdom of God. "Cross" is a metaphor for the Kingdom of God. The [nearest] you come to falling is when you feel like quitting. You're tired and the money's not there. I'm not a fundraiser; I didn't give my life to this to be a fundraiser. We're running real tight financially right now. Some more people are leaving when we need them. We're attempting some more radical things. We've just built a thirty-six thousand square foot teen club. All these unchurched kids are coming for half-pipes and skateboarding. We are bringing good Christian rock groups in. We have a coffeehouse, and game rooms, and a gymnasium; it's huge. I've got some old people walking out, asking, "How are you going to pay the bills?" All I want to do is preach the gospel. You know, I'm not a businessperson.

I'm in Ginghamsburg, Ohio, sixteen miles north of Dayton, which has only one hundred eighty thousand in population. I'm three miles from Tipp City. There's only six thousand people living in Tipp City. Everywhere I look, farm fields surround me. I don't know how I got here, except, "Yes, Jesus." And to say to people around me, "I'm not quitting, follow me." What makes leaders is that we are the first to the front. David was a kid, but he was the leader. Saul had the position...

**Chandler:** But David was the leader.

**Slaughter:** David was the first to the front. David was, in his youth-fulness and everything else, willing to put his behind on the line. First to the front, first to see the need, and first one willing to commit everything he was and is to the success of the mission.

**Chandler:** Therefore, that's your role as pastor: to be first to the front, on the edge. If you're on the growing edge of being teachable by the Holy Spirit every week and willing to take risks with the church, then God will provide.

**Slaughter:** In a typical pastor's office right now, you and I can picture the suit and tie, the hair part, the thirty pounds excess weight, and everything else. We've got the picture of the typical pastor right now. Is it Saul or David? Is it Saul, up on the hill, who understands that the giant that we have to confront, of postmodern paganism, is taunting us to turn to every other spiritual format. We don't know what we should do. Yet we have the *position* of leadership. But David, the leader, probably didn't fit all of the denominational qualifications. But David says, "I'll deliver." It's that leader who is not fearful, who trusts God enough, "Though he slay me, yet will I trust in him" (Job 13:15a, KJV)

I'd rather die trying; I'd rather be the pastor of two hundred folks who are revolutionary followers of Jesus than the CEO of a lukewarm organiza-tion. I'm going to be in people's space every week. What is the product of the revolutionary follower? It's not a big church. It's not attendance. What are the measurements? We start talking about measurements: I've got four thousand people coming to this thing. That's not the measurement. The measurements? I read about Peter: "With your faith, there's goodness, with goodness, mutual affection, with mutual affection, love" (2 Pet. 1:5–7, para-phrase). Those are the measurements I see there.

**Chandler:** Not the ABCs—attendance, buildings, or cash.

**Slaughter:** No, "With this you will provide yourself to be fruitful for God's purposes in the world."

**Chandler:** What are the things you would say to a pastor or lay leader frustrated because their church seems stuck? Change what you measure?

**Slaughter:** Oh, yeah. It's not whether people are pleased with us or happy with us or anything else. But, are we really the hands and feet of Jesus? Are we winning the lost and setting the oppressed free? Everything comes down to that.

There are churches out there made up of ninety people, who are revolutionary and in revolutionary ways are impacting their communities. Other churches of this size may say, "Mike, you should have stayed small, then you were not quite an embarrassment." You didn't do anything else but put my name on what the country club up the street was doing. There's sexism, racism, everything else. Your people reflected a Republican ideology, or Democratic ideology, a conservative ideology, or liberal, rather than the Bible.

**Chandler:** Talk a little bit about your twenty years plus tenure here. Your leadership has, obviously, evolved. What kinds of things have you had to let go of along the way? What have you picked up in their place?

**Slaughter:** You have to know what your sweet spot is. I don't know if you play sports, but while watching my son last night, he hit two home runs. You know when he hits the sweet spot. Sometimes he just doesn't quite get it out of the park. One time I said, "That was a great hit," but he said, "I didn't quite get it." Even if it goes out, he'll say, "I didn't get it." Just the way it feels. If you play tennis you can hit it off the sweet spot and it still goes over the net. It's not the same. In your life as a pastor, if you know your gifts and call, this is your sweet spot. If you live out of that sweet spot, you're going to be energized and blessed. People around you are going to be energized and blessed. If you live outside of your sweet spot, you may be able to get it across the net, but...

**Chandler:** Can you name a few things that are out of your sweet spot?

**Slaughter:** Counseling. I was trained in social work. I was good at counseling. I read conjoint family therapy, reality therapy, and Carl Rogers. I looked over things before people came in, and afterwards, I'd take notes and everything. I did it better probably than average pastors. But it de-energized me. Now, we have the counseling center down on our south campus. We have seven degreed, licensed, mastered counseling folk who do much better than I did. I don't do any counseling.

When I did weddings, which everyone has to do, it de-energized me. I do them well but I put so much into it. God hates divorce, I hate divorce; I feel responsible when I say, "By the authority granted to me by God, I pronounce you man and wife." (I never say state of Ohio because I'm not appointed by the state of Ohio!) Weddings wore me out.

My sweet spot is what I'm doing now: teaching and proclaiming the Kingdom. Instead of doing weddings Saturday and proclaiming Sundays, I want to do proclamation both days. We have licensed laypeople in the church who do the weddings. I can't because I'm preaching. What life would I have if Friday nights, instead of being at my son's football games, I'd be at a wedding rehearsal? I'm a teacher. I'm a teacher-leader-evangelist.

**Chandler:** That's what picks up your pulse.

**Slaughter:** My twenty-second elevator version of my mission statement is, "To connect people to their God-destiny." I do that with everyone I'm with. When I'm doing that, I'm in my sweet spot. When I was in a board meeting yesterday morning at 6:45, talking about a financial situation and fundraising, it de-energized me. I hate fundraising. I hate administration. I am a spiritual leader; I'm not a CEO. I am a spiritual leader and I know that and I'm going to operate out of that sweet spot. I want those other people that have administrative gifts, those pastoral gifts. I don't have pastoral gifts; I have prophetic gifts. My laypeople say my spiritual gift is the gift of irritation [*laughter*].

**Chandler:** Help the pastor who feels the sweet spot is teaching, leading, preaching, planning, evangelizing, but is burdened with other expectations.

**Slaughter:** I wrote about it in my first book, *Spiritual Entrepreneurs.*[3] The sixth chapter is called, "Leadership Is the Difference." I compare Moses as a visionary leader and Aaron as the traditional pastor/manager. Because people who go into ministry tend to be codependent in many ways, what Aaron does (since he doesn't have a clear vision from God) is he becomes a group facilitator, a board-committee person. "Well, what do you all want to do?" He wants to do what you want to do. He does not speak as a clear leader with vision and anointing and authority from God, who says, "This is why we're here, this is what we're going to do, this is how we're going to do it." If you put out the vote, people are always going to vote to go back to the way it has been. That's all they know.

**Chandler:** Better vegetables back in Egypt.

**Slaughter:** That's all they know. What they do stems from their past tradition, the values they bring out of Egypt. As a pastor, the most important thing you can do is get in touch with the vision that God has placed on you. "Why am I here? What am I supposed to do?" I even write about how I went out behind that little country church in April of 1979 and said, "God, I'm not leaving here without a vision of what this is supposed to be." I stayed there all day and began to picture a vision. Then I quite frankly said to the people, "I'm twenty-seven years old. I'm almost dead; life is a bore. You have to trust and believe this is going to work; give it a year."

I taped some meat wrapping paper up on the boards. I said, "Here are some gifts: preaching, teaching, visitation, leadership, involvement in community organizations, anything, weddings." Okay, now list and prioritize. I gave them each a sheet of paper and said, "Write these things down and prioritize: this is important for a staff person. So Dwight, what do you have? You've got visitation as number one. Okay, Dennis, what do you have? Number one is preaching. The first thing I did was show that nine people didn't agree. Then I said, "Here are my gifts. I'm a prophetic teacher, leader, and evangelist. I'm going to focus on these and you all have gifts. I'm going to have you operate under your anointing because when you do that, you do that better. Some of you may have the gift of healing and you need to be the ones to go to nursing homes." We began to do gifts-based ministry. We began to exercise gifts-based ministry versus professional position ministry. It's about empowering the laity to do that.

**Chandler:** Pastors and congregations must understand that the person who holds the office of pastor is not necessarily called by God to be "the pastor," but rather the one who teaches and empowers the pastors in the church to do the pastoral work using their gifts. Then the church is set free

---

[3]Michael Slaughter, *Spiritual Entrepreneurs: 6 Principles for Risking Renewal* (Nashville: Abingdon Press, 1995).

to do ministry and people are able to function by gifts, instead of by title or position.

**Slaughter:** Right.

**Chandler:** What coaching would you do to help congregational leaders learn on your nickel, from a mistake that you made?

**Slaughter**: I have made a lot of mistakes. I didn't put my family before the church. One of the mistakes that we have made as leaders in the church is that we can reflect the way the world does think and operate out of drivenness. We do the same thing as a church. So people don't see the reality of how the Kingdom of God makes us different, how it liberates us. From 1992 to today, my covenant to my wife and family became my priority. I remember one day my son, who was pretty young, had a microphone on the seat next to him, and he picked it up and was kind of playing with it. I could hear him and on the speakers there was static, so I asked my wife, "Would you take that away from him? I'm preaching." He got really upset, started crying, and went out. So, I said, "Hey, you guys, you'll have to excuse me, I've got to go out." So I went outside, sat on the curb, talked to my son.

**Chandler:** In the middle of worship?

**Slaughter:** In the middle of my sermon! I'm out there on the curb. I'm like, "Buddy, I shouldn't have embarrassed you in front of people like that with that mic deal." He was kind of a sensitive kid. I had a crowd of people in there, but I'm not ready to drop my son. Today, he's obedient to Jesus. What I'm seeing is that this kind of investment has made a difference.

**Chandler:** A Kingdom difference.

**Slaughter:** A Kingdom difference. This kid will go to the University of Pennsylvania, knowing who he is and whose he is. He may have some struggles but he's got a grasp of Jesus.

**Chandler:** Your leadership lesson would be for key church leaders to demonstrate and model the Kingdom within their families?

**Slaughter:** Yes. What am I most proud of? My family. Look around at my pictures in this office. I've got a letter over there about working on *The Prince of Egypt,*[4] but that's not what I'm most proud of. It's those pictures of my family. It's that Jesus redeemed my marriage, my family. That's what I'm most proud of.

### Reflecting on the Trip: Questions for Continuing the Conversation

1. Does a church have to lose people in order to awaken to a radical different model and scale of ministry?
2. How can pastors best deal with the ongoing stream of departures from the congregation in a growing church? What is the best way to deal with "Pastor Pigface" letters?

---

[4] *The Prince of Egypt,* directed by Brenda Chapman and Steve Hickner (Glendale, Calif.: DreamWorks SKG, 1998).

3. How can a leadership community reframe the role of the pastor away from acts of "institutional care?" For whom is this more difficult, for pastor or the congregation?
4. What can pastors do to create new leadership pods? How is this more effective than reforming change-resistant individuals and groups? How can a leader tell when a person is coachable toward growth?
5. What should we measure in congregational life? What should we stop measuring?
6. Given the unique status (plight? opportunity?) of spouses and children of pastors, how do pastors move beyond doing lip service as family members vis-à-vis their work in congregational life? How do pastors prevent their entire calling in Christ from being subsumed in their identity as pastor (rather than, for instance, as a parent)? Do pastors have to create and endure great family pain before re-prioritizing, or are there ways of getting it right before pain?

## 7

*Interview with* **Leith Anderson**
Wooddale Church, Eden Prairie, Minnesota
www.wooddale.org

# Courageous Blending

Leith Anderson has been senior pastor of Wooddale Church in Eden Prairie, Minnesota, since 1977. He is author of *Dying for Change*,[1] *A Church for the 21st Century*,[2] *Leadership That Works*,[3] and several other books. Wooddale is a diverse and vibrant congregation. It has planted many churches, including new church starts for denominations other than its own.

### Here's a Trip-tik™ of things to watch for:
✓ The premium on durability, adaptability, and sustainability in leadership decisions, styles, and structures
✓ The ears and eyes of a leader as "sociologist"
✓ How the past—and the future—get to "vote" in decisions
✓ A leadership board that aligned with a young pastor and helped him withstand early storms, leading to a long and fruitful match
✓ Staff meetings that invigorate rather than exhaust
✓ How leaders began to expect more—and receive it—from the congregation
✓ Getting cut on the cutting edge

---

[1]Leith Anderson, *Dying for Change* (Minneapolis: Bethany House, 1990).
[2]Leith Anderson, *A Church for the 21st Century* (Minneapolis: Bethany House, 1992).
[3]Leith Anderson, *Leadership that Works: Hope and Direction for Church and Parachurch Leaders in Today's Complex World* (Minneapolis: Bethany House, 2002).

✓ When to die, when to relocate, or when to couple with a next-level congregation

---

**Chandler:** Your ministry at Wooddale has spanned a quarter of a century. What has been the most remarkable thing you have experienced there?

**Anderson:** Twenty-five years of growth is a significant accomplishment. Many of the questions about our growth are based on the assumption of a crisis or turnaround at some point. Yet I can't think of many crises or turning points. What we have seen at Wooddale Church is the establishment of a structure that is durable. It evolves and changes as it adapts.

**Chandler:** So the church's growth has been more "evolution" than "revolution"?

**Anderson:** Absolutely. We have gone from a traditional to a contemporary church and seen significant growth without alienating many people.

**Chandler:** Was that in the game plan from the beginning or did you stumble onto it? How did you design this "durable structure" to grow?

**Anderson:** A commitment to outreach was paramount. The Doctor of Ministry program at Fuller Theological Seminary was very helpful in the church growth studies with Peter Wagner. After studying church growth, the questions became, not, "How do we become a contemporary church?" or, "How do we offer a different style of worship?" The questions were, "How do we reach people and make them disciples of Jesus Christ? What will it take to do that?" We started to figure that out, not on the basis of the latest trend, but on the basis of doing what needs to be done for evangelism.

**Chandler:** The study of church growth did not become an end in itself, but a means to an end of reaching people, with means that changed over the years?

**Anderson:** Church growth may be classically defined as, "Making more disciples for Jesus Christ." But a secular definition is, "The application of the social sciences to the life of the church." And, it works! It understands, for instance, that strangers in a group of two hundred are not going to interact. However, they will interact in a group of twelve. That's a principle of small group dynamics, whether it's a church, a mosque, a political meeting, whatever. Applying those principles has allowed us to fulfill the mandates of the gospel.

**Chandler:** Your leadership has been as a sociologist as much as a theologian?

**Anderson:** Yes, I have a degree in sociology. That has been helpful for us.

**Chandler:** Wooddale is known, not as a purely contemporary church, but one that has blended contemporary and traditional congregations under one roof. There's a huge pipe organ, people are dressed in formal ways. How have you been able to include people who connect with God in those ways alongside of people who connect with God and each other in more informal, contemporary ways?

**Anderson:** First of all, it's to recognize, sociologically, the demographics of our area. The demographics of our area include people who are professional and educated. A typical resident of our community would have a college education. So there's an intellectual style that permeates what we're doing.

However, there are some things that are common in both the traditional and contemporary. We try to avoid jargon. We don't use many religious terms that would be understood only by those who come from within the church. The way to test that, by the way, is for a Baptist to go into a Catholic or Lutheran church. Realize how often things are said and done that you don't understand.

**Chandler:** For instance?

**Anderson:** When to stand and when to sit. Let's take the Salvation Army for an example. The Salvation Army has "cartridges." Do you know what cartridges are?

**Chandler:** No.

**Anderson:** "Cartridges" are what Southern Baptists call "tithes." The Salvation Army has "soldiers." Do you know what those are?

**Chandler:** Members.

**Anderson:** They have "officers."

**Chandler:** Pastors.

**Anderson:** They don't have "hymns," they have "songs." They have a whole set of terminology. But so do Baptists! So do Episcopalians! If you're intending to reach only Baptists, you can use that type of terminology. You can talk about Lottie Moon and refer to the North American Mission Board. But outsiders have no idea what that means at all.

We have pretty much purged our vocabulary of those types of references. Whether we're in a traditional or contemporary setting, we'll refer to the "Bible" rather than "Scripture." If we talk about Vacation Bible School, we won't say "V.B.S." We'll say, "During this week in the summer, there are classes your children can come to and have a lot of fun." We try to minimize terminology that they don't understand.

**Chandler:** The sociology of the leadership is not to force people to break a code.

**Anderson:** They don't have to learn our jargon. When referring to Bible (not "Scripture") reading, I'll give a page number, not just chapter and verse.

We have also recognized that there are different audiences that need to be reached in different ways, so we have six weekend services: one on

Saturday night and five on Sunday morning. Two of those six are what we would call "traditional," although "traditional" is in the eye and ear of the beholder. What is traditional to some is not traditional to others. Those services include a pipe organ. I wear a suit and tie. Our contemporary services include drums and synthesizers. I'm dressed casually, with slacks and a golf shirt. But we have "liturgical" services, where there's a crucifer, a processional, and I wear a robe. We follow the Book of Common Prayer.

**Chandler:** When the styles vary that widely, what keeps those groups unified under the rubric of "Wooddale Church?" What is the glue or source of common identity?

**Anderson:** In the worship, it's the message or the theme. For the most part, the preacher is the same. Ultimately, it's the common values. We give the Bible page numbers in traditional, contemporary, and liturgical services. An interesting example was the weekend of September 15–16, 2001, following the terrorist bombings of the World Trade Center. In each service, we sang, "A Mighty Fortress Is Our God."[4] In the traditional service, it was with pipe organ and orchestra. It was sung the way people learned it who grew up in Lutheran churches. (Lutheran churches are very common in Minnesota.) In the contemporary services, it was much more rapid, it had a different tune, and was stylistically different.

**Chandler:** Kind of like the original Martin Luther barroom song?

**Anderson:** It was! But the words were identical in each service. There's a lot of similarity, but also dissimilarity. The wonderful thing is that people will switch back and forth. People will go to one style because other members of their family prefer that style. We are also discovering something I would not have anticipated; that is, the growing interest in traditional and liturgical worship is in those who are younger, not those who are older.

**Chandler:** Why is that?

**Anderson:** I don't think we know the answer yet. But it may be that what we have termed "contemporary" music is really a baby boomer phenomenon. That's not to say that it's going to pass and we're going to go back to singing John and Charles Wesley songs. It is to say that what comes next may be distinctive to future generations. Our younger generation is, in many ways, more conservative. It is attracted to mystery and the mystique of yesterday, whereas our baby boomers have less concern for yesterday. They have less respect for those who went before.

**Chandler:** If you find within a single household that different people connect with God through different worship styles, how then do you minister to those different people so that they feel as if they're connecting with God?

---

[4]Martin Luther wrote this classic hymn in 1529, and Frederick H. Hedge translated its lyrics in 1852. See *Chalice Hymnal,* ed. Daniel B. Merrick (St. Louis: Chalice Press, 1995), no. 65.

**Anderson:** The real question you are raising is not how they are connecting with God; it's, "How are they connecting with each other if they're speaking seemingly different languages?" The answer is that there are enough similarities; there is enough common ground. Protestant worship in America in general has commonalities. Interestingly, recently I read in a newspaper article that mosques in the United States have a different style of worship than mosques in the Middle East, because they have adopted so many Protestant American church styles. Many Roman Catholic churches sing the same songs we're singing in Protestant churches. If you never step over the line into someone else's church culture, you may not understand how many similarities are there.

**Chandler:** A sort of "American worship style"?

**Anderson:** In Anglo churches, for example, services are typically an hour or an hour and fifteen minutes. African American services are typically longer. That's a cultural style. If somebody is planting an African American church and planning to have fifty-minute services, it's going to be out of line with the cultural expectation. The opposite is also true. I think we have a lot of expectations in American Protestantism: we sing, we have a speech, we generally sit in rows that face the front, there is often professional clergy...all of these are pretty well understood. There are obvious exceptions. But these expectations permeate most of our churches, regardless of style.

**Chandler:** You recently quoted the G. K. Chesterton saying "Tradition means giving votes to the most obscure of all classes, our ancestors."[5] Has your experience been that it is more difficult to ensure that the past gets a vote, or making sure the past doesn't get too many of the votes?

**Anderson:** Well, at Wooddale Church, we have focused on the unchurched and the underchurched. We have many people who don't bring church baggage. We have people who are unaware of the past. We don't have many people who are saying, "Let's do it the way we used to do it."

**Chandler:** Was there an earlier time when that wasn't so? Was there some critical point when there were now more of the new folk than those who had preceded you, who had always been here?

**Anderson:** Yes, I once calculated what I believed was the precise date! Sure, during the first years I was at the church, most people had been there longer than I had been there. Then, there was attrition as some of those people left because they didn't like me or didn't like what the church was doing. New people came. Unfortunately, for a couple of years more people left than came! Eventually, the hemorrhage stopped, and new people kept coming. They understood the vision and style and said, "This is what we want." That was a wonderful turning point.

---

[5]This saying was part of a 1908 article from a publication titled *Orthodoxy*. For this and other G. K. Chesterton's quotations, visit www.chesterton.org.

**Chandler:** What carried you through the hemorrhage?

**Anderson:** Leadership.

**Chandler:** Your personal leadership or the leadership of the church?

**Anderson:** The members of the church board resolved that I was the person that they were convinced God had called. They were going to stand by me in unanimity even if others left.

**Chandler:** So you knew you would have a church of no fewer than nine?

**Anderson:** Seven of them and two of us! Probably if it had gotten that bad, they would have left, too. I actually believe that's one of the reasons we are where we are today. Those leaders were convinced that I was the right person. There was very much a sense that they were shaping me for what they wanted, and probably far less of a sense that I was shaping the church.

**Chandler:** Speak to that a little more.

**Anderson:** I think they wanted a church that was relevant and outreaching. They went out and contacted me—I was thirty-one years old—and said, "This guy has enough experience, but we can make him into what we want him to be."

**Chandler:** Therefore, a young whippersnapper did not import the vision for Wooddale; it resided in the people. Their calling you to be pastor was a matter of matching your gifts with the dream that was already there.

**Anderson:** The *seeds* of it were there. The church had gone through a very difficult time with the previous pastor leaving. Some strong lay leadership spoke up and were given further leadership. They went out to find somebody who could fulfill what was an *emerging* vision. Here's what happened: I didn't know much of what I was doing. They knew more of what they were doing. We got together and they shaped me. Eventually, the lay leadership changed and I emerged as a stronger leader. There has been somewhat of a reallocation of authority. Nonetheless, we are still a lay-led church. It's interesting. I'll still have conversations with people who say, "What's the highlight of your week, or month?" Two of the highlights are the board meeting and the church staff meeting.

**Chandler:** Why is that?

**Anderson:** There's unanimity. We're the same on values and vision. There's never a sense of acrimony or criticism. There's a sense of, "We can do this, and let's do this together." It's exhilarating! Our staff meetings are Monday mornings at eight o'clock. One of the reasons is that when you're tired and weary after Sunday, you need something to invigorate you. Staff meetings invigorate me.

**Chandler:** Somehow, you've created a sense of collaboration between pastor, staff, and people. There's a synergy that refreshes everyone it touches.

**Anderson:** We once got an interesting question from someone on our pastoral staff: was he allowed to come to pastoral staff meetings while he was on vacation? He didn't want to miss it. I think that's exactly the way it should be. What's attendance at board meetings? It's usually one hundred per cent. Of course it is; nobody wants to miss.

**Chandler:** Would you describe your leadership role as "climate control," in creating a culture where that kind of exciting, excited leadership flourishes?

**Anderson:** Very much so. Lyle Schaller says that Wooddale is a "high expectation" church. We expect people to come to meetings. We expect them to invite other people to come to church. We expect them to pray. We expect them to give. Those expectations permeate everything we do. When new people come, even if they have no church background at all or they've never been in church before, they learn quickly because everyone around you expects you to do these things. In a low-expectation church, only half of the people show up for board meetings.

**Chandler:** Can you describe the evolution of becoming this kind of high-expectation church? Certainly you didn't just march in as a thirty-one year old and announce these high expectations.

**Anderson:** Having consistent standards and applying them fairly is important. One of the most difficult places to apply high expectations is in music. We have an expectation that people hit the notes, connect emotionally, have good doctrine, and you can understand what they sing. Suppose you have a soloist who's been singing for years and can't meet those expectations. Well, then that person doesn't sing. When you're new, it's hard to get that type of change to take place. We tried to give people an early taste of success. People like it when they have a high expectation and it's met. It's about recruiting volunteers, explaining what it's about, and saying, "We will help you meet this expectation." If the expectation is not unreasonable and they meet it, then they welcome the opportunity for an even higher expectation that they will also be able to meet. When that is done with five people, or ten people, it permeates the church; you then have a high-expectation church. The other factor is: we do not reward dysfunction. If someone is a critic, we deal with that person one on one. We don't allow them to spread their criticism to the rest of the church by giving them a forum.

**Chandler:** You dealt with the off-key soloist by bringing in nine other on-key soloists who raised the bar, and that took care of the tenth? They either rose to a new level or stepped down?

**Anderson:** The really practical answer to that particular issue is that we said, "We want the body to minister." Therefore almost all of the music we do is group music, not individual music. That way, you eliminated having many soloists. But it was also a way of saying, "This is a clear expectation."

**Chandler:** You've said publicly that you're not interested in being a "cutting-edge" church. Can you elaborate on that?

**Anderson:** The counsel is that people should not look to be cutting edge. They should let somebody else be cutting edge, and then go in second or third, and benefit from the lessons learned by others.

**Chandler:** What's wrong with the cutting edge?

**Anderson:** That's where you get cut! Very few people can stay there. Few churches have the resources. Some mushrooms are poisonous and some are not. Someone on the cutting edge found out, "This mushroom kills you"…and died! So, they're dead, but that's very helpful to you. You now know not to eat that particular type of mushroom.

The other side, to be fair, is that Wooddale is, in many ways, a cutting-edge church. We are the only church I know of, in two thousand years, who has voluntarily started churches of other denominations. In the last few years, we've started a Christian Reformed church, and a Southern Baptist church. We're in conversation with several other denominations now. Hardly anyone—perhaps no one—has ever done that. It's very difficult, very unusual; that was cutting edge. But how many churches can do that? Most churches don't have the resources or the corporate resolve to attempt something so difficult. That's fine. What they ought to do is be "early adopters" with higher levels of success.

**Chandler:** The second one doesn't take the abuse of the cutting edge.

**Anderson:** Think of it in terms of the stock market. If you have ten thousand dollars to invest, you can be on the cutting edge, and lose it all. But you might get one hundred percent return. What if you could always be second or third, and always get a fifty percent return? I'd rather get fifty percent return than risk losing everything.

**Chandler:** In today's market, I'd settle for ten percent!

**Anderson:** Right now, you settle for zero and hope you don't lose it all! I heard an investor recently say that his goal for his clientele was "zero."

**Chandler:** That may actually be an appropriate expectation for some churches.

**Anderson:** Several years ago, in what's called the "Iron Range" of Minnesota, a northern area where there's a lot of iron ore, there was significant decline due to the closing of iron mines. There was 85 percent unemployment. Beautiful homes were selling for low prices. People were leaving town. A church there that was only declining by 10 or 20 percent was fabulous. You've got to measure it by the context. If a congregation is growing by 10 percent in a suburb where other churches are growing by 200 percent, the congregation is underperforming. It's contextual.

**Chandler:** Many of our pastors and churches are "stuck." They can't get past growth barriers, old baggage, church dysfunction, or competency limitations. Early in your ministry at Wooddale, you and the church got "unstuck." You survived the hemorrhaging and are now thriving. What counsel or word of hope could you give to church leaders who are in a "stuck" situation and want to see God's future beyond it?

**Anderson:** Some churches are stuck, are going to stay stuck, and might as well stay stuck, because they're not going to change. They might as well live as best they can with what they've got. Other churches need to call Pastor Kevorkian, die, go out of business, and be done. Other churches can and should change. I think there are specific things they can do. One is to relocate. Probably 10 percent of the churches in America should sell their buildings and move. They're no longer where they can reach people. The buildings are laden with asbestos. There's no disability access. There are ump-teen reasons why they ought to relocate. Churches that relocate often have whole new chapters of life ahead of them. As an interesting aside, senior pastors who are with churches when they relocate tend to take on roles much like a founding pastor has with a church, which is much different than a successor pastor.

**Chandler:** If relocation is not an option, what's the first, best step toward getting unstuck?

**Anderson:** The single best thing for churches who want to change is to spend a day on the telephone finding a church that was, five years ago, pretty much like your church: similar size, similar dysfunction, and similar community. But this church has addressed those issues and moved to a size where you would one day like to be. Go visit that church with eight or ten of the most influential leaders in your congregation. The rules of thumb are: (1) the farther away, the better; and (2) drive, don't fly—because the transformation takes place on the ride home. People sit in the car and say, "We could never do it." Then someone else says, "They did it, and they're just like us." That beats seminars and books, because you can actually see it and ask the questions.

**Chandler:** Find a next-level church, get key lay leaders on board, and process that together as a leadership team.

**Anderson:** Right. But if it's a church of one hundred, the "next level church" is probably not Willow Creek.[6] It's a church of two or three hundred people. Many church leaders go to a megachurch conference and say on the way home, "We don't want that to happen. They'll kick us out. We won't be part of that church." Then they become resistant to that change. But if they see change that they like, then they're going to adapt and adopt.

**Chandler:** Not every person in a church of one hundred wants to be fifteen thousand, but most of them would want to be in a church of at least one hundred and fifty.

**Anderson:** Or they would at least like to survive at one hundred. You're exactly right: they need to find the place where they want to go. It should be incremental. A friend who grew up on a dairy farm in Wisconsin had five siblings. He said, "One of the best things Mother ever did was to have us one at a time, because if she'd had us all six the same day, we

---

[6]The church's Web site is www.willowcreek.org.

never would have gotten the cows milked. It would have ruined the farm. But by spreading all six out, two years apart, it worked." That's true of most churches. They should do change incrementally.

## Reflecting on the Trip: Questions for Continuing the Conversation

1. How can the field of church growth (the application of the social sciences to congregational life) be a useful discipline for leaders? How do leaders avoid the extremes of ignoring its findings or lionizing church growth as the "be-all-end-all solution for" the congregation?
2. Leith suggests attending services of different denominations as a way of unearthing jargon in one's own congregation. What are other ways leaders can audit and improve the intelligibility of congregational life for the benefit of newcomers exploring it?
3. How can the pastor be a "resident of the church" and be shaped by the congregation rather than simply trying to shape the congregation?
4. What would it take to create staff and board meetings so magnetic that people interrupt vacations to be a part of them?
5. Lyle Schaller speaks of a continuum between "voluntary association" and "high expectation" congregations.[7] Leith mentions that one way Wooddale moved toward the "high expectation" end was rigorous application with respect to music. What is an immediate area in your congregation that needs to be held under the light of higher expectations?
6. How can leaders help churches avoid the unnecessary pain and risk of edgy innovation without incurring the opportunity costs of being "middle adopters"?
7. Who are the congregations that are one or two steps ahead of yours? How can you couple with and learn from them?

---

[7]See, for example, Lyle Schaller, *44 Questions for Congregational Self-Appraisal* (Nashville: Abingdon Press, 1998).

## 8

*Interview with* **Lance Watson**
The Saint Paul's Baptist Church, Richmond, Virginia
www.myspbc.org

# Courageous Alliances

Lance Watson is pastor of The Saint Paul's Baptist Church in Richmond, Virginia, and author of *Maximize Your Edge.*[1]

As a sweeping generalization, Virginia is a history-focused, tradition-honoring, and culturally conservative commonwealth. The capitol city of Richmond amplifies those characteristics. And "Church Hill," where Patrick Henry said, "*Give me liberty or give me death,*" is a traditional neighborhood within this traditional city. Into this neighborhood context in 1985 Lance Watson came from Detroit. One of the most captivating speakers in North America, Lance has led the church through numerous stages of growth, multiple relocations, and into an expanding national ministry. This has happened not only through his immense personal gifts, but also through sustained attention to developing partnerships and alliances with long-term and emerging leaders in the church.

### Here's a Trip-tik™ of things to watch for:
✓ How to learn through failure and critique early in ministry
✓ Setting congregational leaders free to dream in playful ways, creating leadership communities and amplifying vision
✓ Creative ways of motivating people through helping them to remember and name the vision God has for the congregation

---

[1]Lance D. Watson, *Maximize Your Edge: Navigating Life's Challenges* (New Kensington, Pa.: Whitaker House, 2001).

✓ Breaking congregational inertia through creating new dialogues instead of revisiting dead-end conversations or issues

✓ Releasing burdensome ministry tasks into the hands of other passionately called and equipped ministers; developing other leaders develops your own ability to lead

---

**Chandler:** Tell me what you saw when you arrived at Saint Paul's.

**Watson**: I came in September 1985 and was installed as pastor in 1986. What I saw? I had some reticence about wanting to come, only because (like most churches), it needed *so* much and I didn't have a clue as to where to begin. I did what I had been doing. I came in and preached, did a little bit of visitation, taught Bible study, and tried to encourage the people. But the first part of my journey there was a kind of wandering, because I didn't have a clue, in terms of what I was doing, or what we could do together.

**Chandler**: You obviously saw enough there to warrant coming, enough resident potential that led you to say, "Maybe we can go somewhere together as pastor and people."

**Watson**: Interestingly, I received a letter from one of the members. The church extended a call, and I didn't respond for a whole month. They didn't even get a phone call from me. But a member wrote a letter, and said, that she had been in this church her whole life. She said, "I realize that as you look at us, there may not seem like there's much potential. But I would encourage you to pray about it. We believe that you are the one God has for us. And we're willing to work with you, because we believe that, together, we can do great things." I still have that letter.

**Chandler**: So her sense of vision sparked your imagination to wonder, "What if it's true?"

**Watson**: It pushed me over the edge. Because, to be perfectly honest, I was fresh out of seminary, and had bright-eyed visions of wanting to go to churches that had already "arrived." In retrospect, I praise God for the Spirit's leadership, because I was not ready for a church of thousands. I didn't know that I wasn't ready; I thought I was. But I was not ready for that level of leadership. It probably would have killed me: the exertion of energy, the frustration of ministry, and experiencing major failure right at the very beginning. I just didn't have the discipline, focus, skill, and stamina to be able to sustain leadership at that level. It's only in looking back that I now recognize that.

**Chandler**: So, you went and did the things pastors do, for a season.

**Watson**: Right.

**Chandler**: Then, at some point, something happened that caused you to decide that if you were going to a higher level as a church, you were going to have to do some things differently as a church.

**Watson**: Right.

**Chandler:** Would you describe that?

**Watson**: There was a definite turning point. I had been preaching evangelistically since age twelve. Therefore, when I first came, my ministry was mostly evangelistic. I was the kind of person who wants to witness, wants to see people come to the Lord, and see people change. So that hallmark was there, right from the beginning. I was talking about reaching out and touching people's lives. But I was clueless in terms of moving an organization, or getting a group of people to buy into that. From September 1985 to February 1986, *nobody* joined the church. I went home every Sunday crying the blues to my wife in the car: "I hope this isn't a Jeremiah ministry— gonna preach my whole life and never get one convert; people gonna throw me in the pit," and all of that. She listened patiently. The very next Sunday, when I was installed in the church, one lady came down and joined, so that was some encouragement. But in all honesty, from the time I came until 1987, I wandered in the wilderness. If you had asked me, "What is your vision for this church?" I couldn't have told you, because I didn't have one.

**Chandler:** "To preach next Sunday…"

**Watson**: Right. That was my vision: to have a good sermon next Sunday. However, some good things were happening. A woman came to me after I'd been there a year. She gave me a critique, which I took as criticism. She said, "There's something wrong with your sermons." I replied, "What?" She responded, "You present an excellent case. You never ask for the sale." As it turns out, she was a very successful insurance agent. That criticism proved to be very productive. In every message, I began to think about that, because it was seared into me.

The turning point was this: I had been watching Robert Schuller. And in January 1987, I decided to go to his "Institute for Successful Church Management" with one of my associates. That was an absolutely life-changing week at the Crystal Cathedral. Absolutely. When I came back, my direction was set. I had an idea of what was possible. What had intrigued me about Robert Schuller was the book, *Tough Times Never Last, But Tough People Do,*[2] in which he tells the story of the progression of his ministry. I'm saying to myself, "Yeah, 1950s, but this is the eighties, going into the nineties, I don't know if this is doable now." But going out there, seeing it, then having the opportunity to interact with him accidentally (or, I should say, "providentially")–this was really beneficial.

One question he asked in our five minutes together. I'm walking around his office, looking at his books, having cajoled one of his secretaries to let me in. And he walks in. I introduced myself; he asked me about my ministry.

---

[2] Robert Schuller, *Tough Times Never Last, But Tough People Do!* (Nashville: Thomas Nelson, 1983).

I said, I'm clueless: "Well, I'm doing this, I don't really know…" He said, "Let me ask you a question: What would you do for God if you knew you could not fail?" I didn't have an answer for that, because my mind-set at that time was not focused on functioning without the fear of failure. I was simply trying to avoid failing: "What if nobody joins? What if we don't meet the budget?" All of my thoughts about ministry were conditioned by the thoughts of failure. That question really just haunted me all the way back. Because when he saw me struggling with that, he said, "Because that *is* what we preach, that God never fails."

**Chandler**: A woman in the church sparked your imagination, another woman in the church critiqued your ministry, and these things helped to create both intrigue and dissatisfaction with ministry as a series of week-to-week activities with no discernible vision.

**Watson**: Right.

**Chandler**: Then you went to a leadership/motivational event, and there, that restlessness got a "true north" question that helped you think about ministry as something visionary, something more than week-to-week acts.

**Watson**: Exactly! It resulted in a self-motivated track of learning. When I came back, I was like a treasure hunter in the bookstore. Searching for books on vision, mission, objectives, management, and leadership. Inundating myself with tapes from Willow Creek, Saddleback,[3] anywhere I can find it. I'm reading Carl George,[4] George Barna,[5] and Elmer Towns. I was just trying to get a fix on what was missing. I felt that what was missing was this clearly discernible vision of why God had placed me *here*, at this time, with these people. After that time, for three or four months, absorbing all this, I decided to have my own, smaller version of the "Institute for Successful Church Management" at the church. A two-day leadership retreat for all the key leadership people in the church, both those who had offices and those who were just "influence" kind of personalities. We had a leadership retreat in Richmond. The first night, I gave a three-sentence keynote address. The opening was, "What would you do for God if you knew you could not fail?" The most powerful things happened; that question freed them to dream. In that moment, I understood what Jesus meant when he said, "Except you become as little children, you cannot enter the Kingdom." Until you are free to dream apart from the fear of failure, you can never see what God might potentially do in your situation. I set them free by saying, "We're gonna dream. We're gonna play. We're gonna be children before the Lord, so we can see what the Lord has for us to do." We

---

[3]The church's Web site is www.saddleback.com.

[4]Carl F. George, *Prepare Your Church for the Future* (Grand Rapids: Revell, 1991). See also George's book with Warrren Bird, *How to Break Growth Barriers* (Grand Rapids: Baker Book House, 1993).

[5]George Barna has written dozens of books, such as *The Habits of Highly Effective Churches* (Ventura, Calif.: Regal Books, 1999).

ended the night by going to get ice cream. What I discovered that weekend was that their vision was much bigger than anything I had ever imagined. All laypeople. I broke them into small groups, and they began to dream about what type of church we would create. They came back with stuff that frightened *me*! "We'll do this, have that…!" We condensed those things to one sheet of paper at the end, and that became our working document for how we were going to go about becoming this church.

**Chandler:** Did you get any help at that point?

**Watson**: We were affiliated with the Richmond Baptist Association. So we had this programmatic model: Sunday school, Women's Missionary Union, Brotherhood, etc. We began working this programmatic model with all-out intensity. We wanted to become an attractive church, increasing in numbers. That was in everyone's comments. We wanted to have something for everybody. One of the metaphors was, "We no longer want to be 7–11." What we wanted to be was "Regency Mall." We wanted to have some strong anchors, and then hundreds of specialty stores."

**Chandler**: A "seven-days-a-week" church.

**Watson**: Yes. People could come from a long distance and it would be worthwhile. "7–11" is the kind of place you only go to in an emergency. Everything's overpriced.

**Chandler**: You're willing to pay five dollars for a gallon of milk because you need it right now.

**Watson**: But you wouldn't go there every day or week. You hope don't have to, but it's good to know it's there, in case you ever need it. So our concept changed: we began to think of Sunday school, men's ministry, women's ministry, as our "anchor stores." Worship as our anchor. In the metaphor, the anchor provided a quality experience that would reach out into the area. Then we have all of these specialties. At that time, we thought of singles and couples ministries as "specialty" stores; they didn't apply to everyone but certainly met somebody's need.

**Chandler:** I'm struck by the sense of vision that Saint Paul's would be a regional church, not just a local church, and that you didn't have to import that vision from the outside. You simply had to ask the right questions and create the right forums in which the *people's* vision could be unlocked and expressed. It was *their* vision as a congregation, and your leadership seems to be a matter of helping them to express and shape that vision.

**Watson**: Along the way, I became the primary facilitator of the vision. The vision was not something I brought to them. It was something we discovered together; a picture of the possible. My role became to convince and encourage them that it was within reach; to remind them of the God we serve.

**Chandler:** So instead of being the guru or expert CEO, your task is to nurture the faith of the people until they look at God and ask God, "What are you trying to do?" You become a spiritual director.

**Watson**: Exactly. That allowed me to keep my hair from turning gray. I don't want to say that this change has made it easy, because ministry has a lot of challenges. But it has helped me keep my hair, because this role is not saturated with responsibilities. I'm just the facilitator.

**Chandler:** It's not all up to you to find and create the vision.

**Watson**: Nehemiah says that in the beginning, people needed to be reminded of the vision every twenty-six days. And in the beginning, their belief in what was possible was so conditioned by what *had* happened, that it was a struggle to get them to believe from week to week. The smallest thing was a reason for them to be discouraged. As a leader, part of the price that had to be paid was the exertion of energy put into research in developing ways to motivate them. Every group is unique; one group is motivated by one thing, another by another. Some people are motivated visually and some are conceptual learners. Part of my responsibility as a leader was to search out, "What is it that would motivate *these* people?" That took me to their history. I began to search their seventy-six year history for places where significant things had happened. I use them as anchors about what *could* happen down the line.

**Chandler**: Spiritual markers.

**Watson**: Yes. They became my sermon illustrations. I became acquainted with people in their history who were important. Who were their mothers, fathers, neighbors, and community? What was their struggle? And then say, "Can't you see these twelve stones? They already are part of your history."

**Chandler**: The vision by itself was not enough to sustain them every week, and part of your leadership was to give them a broader track record of how this vision was already in progress, through the history of the church? To help them see where it was going to go by helping them see where it already had been?

**Watson**: Right. A slide show was supremely effective. I don't even remember where I got the idea, because it was early nineties, before the big multimedia boom in the church. We did a slide show, set to music and narration. The title of the three-camera slide show was, "A People Called Saint Paul's." I fished around for photos of their families and their church history. I wrote a script and set it to instrumental music—Hubert Laws playing "Amazing Grace" on the flute. We had these dissolving photos of people in the church, faces they knew. Some were present, some had gone on to heaven, some children, some elderly, some families. You heard "Oohs!" and, "That's my grandmother!" I began to talk about Richmond, Richmond's history, what kind of place this is, and what had happened here. I also spoke about how this church was born in 1909, in New Town; about the people who brought it into existence; and what they were about. All of that is research. It is exegesis, the people as well as the text.

**Chandler**: Helping the church to envision its future by remembering its history.

**Watson**: Exactly. There's an African word, pronounced *sankofa,* which means you cannot see the future without first seeing your past. Based on that principle, we created this multimedia presentation. I used the previous pastors as "anchors," and talked about each administration. Got to my own, beginning in 1985, talked about it in a humorous way, talked about some of the things we were presently experiencing.

**Chandler:** What was your administration about?

**Watson**: In the early ministry especially, it was about relationships. Even now, pastoring, for me, is about relationships. It can't be rushed, can't be hurried. It takes time and energy. In the early part of the ministry, I spent a lot of time eating with them, hanging out with them, doing things, taking boat rides, going fishing, and riding on the bus. I had this thing with all my seniors, all twelve of them! We called it "Senior Safari." Once a month, I met with them and took them on an adventure. They never knew where they were going. This was unusual for our seniors, because they're not into adventure; they're into stability! But they were like, "Okay, we've got to go play with our pastor; he's a young guy."

**Chandler:** "Our child…"

**Watson**: Yeah, "So we gotta take care of our child." That was the relationship they developed with me. Even now, all these years in, they still have that rapport with me, despite that there are thousands of people.

**Chandler**: And you're a grown man.

**Watson**: But when they speak from the pulpit on special days or announcements, they'll say, "This is my son, I'm looking out for him, and I think he needs some rest. So I'm telling y'all, the pastor is going on vacation, and leave him alone, don't call him!" In the beginning, the idea was to connect this history of faith with the vision of the future.

I'll never forget, I preached a sermon at this critical intersection, called "Yesterday's Dialogue with Tomorrow." It was on our church anniversary. There were three voices talking in the sermon. First, "yesterday" talked about how good it had been. Then "tomorrow" spoke about how good it could be. Then the sermon ended with "today" talking, saying, "But if something doesn't happen today…if we don't see the vision today…if we don't do this today…then you can't live, tomorrow, and you were in vain, yesterday."

**Chandler**: The ghosts of Christmas past and Christmas future.

**Watson**: It was a pivotal moment. God gave me that word for "right then." In the beginning, there was a lot of investment of energy and time required from me to get it moving. The church was inert, circling itself. To break that inertia required heavy investment. That investment continued unabated for about ten years.

**Chandler**: For ten years, you had to maintain a highly relational ministry in order to help the church get past its historical resistance to the vision of what it could become.

**Watson**: And to be able to put the pains, problems, pressures, and predicaments of the past in some kind of perspective. Even when I came, they very much wanted to live in the administration of the previous pastor, and to get me to respond to issues that were raised there. The church had a chasm related to issues from that time, and they were trying to draw me into that discussion. I had to resist it while creating a new dialogue. Once the church started growing, my highly relational leadership style created problems. I did not make adjustments in my leadership style. I just continued to give more energy (relationally) in response to the growth of the church. I worked up to ninety hours a week, spending literally forty to fifty hours in the office. I was preaching three times every Sunday. One Sunday, I preached five times. I promised God the Father, Son, and Holy Spirit, Jesus, the twelve disciples and ten other responsible people that I'd *never* do that again, as long as the Lord gives me breath! Preaching all the time...then two classes I taught on Monday...two classes on Tuesday...mid-week worship...counseling, twenty to twenty-four appointments a week... writing sermons...doing meetings.

**Chandler:** Something had to give.

**Watson**: Something had to give.

**Chandler**: What gave?

**Watson**: Well, *I* did! At the ten-year mark, I was completely burned out. I had neglected myself, my own self-renewal, rejuvenation. No vacation. Maybe I had this naïve idea that I would somehow be supernaturally rejuvenated and not need rest, "because I was doing the Lord's work," right? So after neglecting myself like that, no down time at all, I was probably sixty pounds overweight. My life was church, a little bit of family, eating, preaching, sleeping, and trying to build this ministry. I just got past my point of endurance.

**Chandler:** What broke the cycle?

**Watson**: I never will forget. I was on a plane to Germany. It was the first isolated block of time I'd had in years. It was a nine-hour flight. I was reading a book, *Ordering Your Private World*, by Gordon McDonald.[6] He used this illustration that got all under my skin. It was a parallel between King Saul and John the Baptist, and their understanding of their ministries. It came to me that, for all the energy I was exerting, I was functioning like Saul. I had *become* my ministry, and lost my personhood in the process. I was "Pastor Watson" when I lay in bed at night. I had ceased to be "Lance Watson." Everywhere I went I was the pastor. Every thought I had was about being the pastor.

**Chandler:** Your entire Christian life subsumed in being the pastor.

---

[6]Gordon McDonald, *Ordering Your Private World,* rev. ed. (Nashville: Thomas Nelson, 2003).

**Watson**: That's right. When I'm relating to my children, they're relating to the pastor. I'm analyzing them and counseling them, not as "Dad." I should have picked it up, because my wife would say things to me like, "I'm not just one of your members; I'm your *wife!*" But I was so absorbed in that mindset, wanting to do a good job, offering an excellent sacrifice to the Lord, that I lost my sense of balance. So I'm sitting there on the plane, convicted in my heart. The way the parallel plays out in the book, McDonald says, is that the reason Saul attempted to assassinate David is that he had confused his position with his personhood. When David showed up as the rightful successor to his position, rather than mentor him, he tried to assassinate him. He saw him, not as a protégé, but as a threat to his personhood. He echoed the phrase about Saul being "one head above everyone else" (in terms of his height; see 1 Sam. 10:23); how that was kind of a play on words by the writer of Scripture that Saul was "one head too big." I was convicted because I saw myself there. The ministry I was working so hard to build was congealing only around me. If I were extracted from the process, by rapture, death, or whatever, it would dissolve.

**Chandler**: There would be no ministry left.

**Watson**: None. This was 1995. Ten years in.

**Chandler**: Has not most of St. Paul's growth as a church taken place since that time? Average attendance in 1985 was two hundred fifty people; in 2001 it was five thousand; in 2006 it's eight thousand.

**Watson**: Oh yeah! In my tenth year, we took in seven hundred people. It didn't matter because I was trying to figure out how to resign. I was empty; I didn't have any more. I had no joy in worship or preaching, nor any of those other things; I was just empty. I didn't know it at the time, but remember the text, "The steps of a good man are ordered by the LORD…" (and this is the part I never read) "…though he fall, he shall not be utterly cast down" (Ps. 37:23–24, KJV). I found redemption there, in that phrase. In our weakness, God is able to teach us things we are unable to receive in our strength.

So in my bitter complaint, and it was a bitter complaint, I said: "I'm out here working for you, feeling this way, going through this!" All the while, these significant life events: in 1995, my oldest kid graduated high school; in 1995, my wife graduated college, after putting her whole career and educational pursuit on hold to rear our children. Within a month of graduating, she had an invitation to tour abroad, doing musical theatre. So I've got all of this changing around me, and I'm saying, "God, I thought you were taking care of all of this!" My whole life was changing and I had no inner resource to deal with it. No emotional reserve to make an adjustment.

**Chandler**: No "spiritual capital."

**Watson**: Right, so I'm seeing all of these things as terminations. Wondering, "How am I going to sustain a marriage with my wife five thousand miles away? What am I going to do now that my kids are leaving?" I knew the ministry was maxxed out. We were cresting at twenty-five hundred people. Yet, I didn't have any more to give. I was inundated.

**Chandler**: At 2,501, you were going to break.

**Watson**: Oh yeah. That would have been the last straw. I had nothing on the inside. In my bitter complaint to God, I said, "Why are you putting this on me? Why do I have to do this? Won't you help me?" You know the response I got back? (I wrote it down.) The only response, one phrase: "I never asked you to do it. *You* wanted to do it. All by yourself."

**Chandler**: "So I let you."

**Watson**: Indeed. That's exactly what had happened. I'm thumbing through the Bible, trying to make sense of it. I get to Moses' prayer, where he's complaining and hollering to God about what he's going through. The Lord responds, "You do not have to bear it alone. Find me seventy. Bring them to me. And the Spirit that's in you, I will put on them" (Num. 11:16–30, paraphrase) Now, God did even more than that for me. I didn't even have to find the people. People saw that I wasn't the guy they knew. They didn't know what was wrong or what had happened. But God raised up the leadership that had been there all along.

**Chandler:** You were too broken to do one more ministry task, finding leaders. Through your brokenness, God brought the leaders needed to carry the church to a whole new dimension.

**Watson**: What I discovered was that I didn't have to do it by myself. They were just letting me do it because I wanted to do it, and because I never asked for help. I'd just take on more and more—classes, sermons, trying to do it all. So when I came to them and said, point blank (and this is a real transition point in our church), "It's too hard for me to visit everybody's who's sick," their immediate response was, "Pastor, we're going to take that from you. We will visit everybody, every month. If there's anybody you need to see, we'll call."

**Chandler**: My sense is that many pastors are at the point where you described yourself: empty, broken, feeling betrayed or abandoned by God, because the ministry is so hard. Their churches are stuck because *they're* stuck. What counsel would you give to a pastor who feels that way, so that they don't have to get to the point where they're absolutely spent. Or do they have to be absolutely spent before this can happen?

**Watson**: I'm not sure. Somebody with my personality had to be absolutely spent in order to receive that blessing. Because my personality—and I think a lot of pastors have personalities like this—says, "I'm going to do everything I can possibly do." Motivated by ambition, guilt, devotion… probably all of these at some point or another…I am going to *make* this happen." Coming out of that experience, I had a number of significant lessons. One, I didn't have to do it by myself. Two, the most important use of my time was to invest in leadership. I didn't realize that.

**Chandler:** Invest in your own leadership, or in developing other leaders?

**Watson:** Primarily developing others, because working to develop them would also develop me. That became my commitment when I came out of all this. I was going to work on pastoring, developing, shepherding, and leading the leadership. Then I was going to release them with both power and authority to do ministry among the membership. That was exactly what I did. To create systems, processes of accountability, fellowship, instruction, and nurture. I released people to do ministry.

**Chandler:** What was difficult about this?

**Watson:** It forced me to deal with my own insecurity. Talking about releasing brings up a lot of insecurity. "What if somebody becomes powerful? What if someone works against me?" You have to deal with all those insecurities. In dealing with my own insecurity, I came to the assurance that this ultimately belongs to God. What God has for me is for me. I am here by divine appointment. God is in this, and it is not a permanent assignment. I'm a "temp" worker! Even if I'm here thirty years, I'm just a temp. Then God will bring in someone else who will also be just a temp. It is not necessary to get all tied up in that power dynamic. My call and focus is to cultivate Christlike leadership, to lift Christ up as the example we follow. "Follow the pastor as he follows the master."

**Chandler:** How do you develop those leaders?

**Watson:** My investment is that every first Saturday, I have an event called "Leadership Summit," which runs ten months a year. In it, I do intentional leadership development. That summit grew out of my time of burnout. It's a time to cast vision, to help them problem-solve. At other levels of leadership, they run into the same things I had. Therefore, I become their coach. The idea now is that I want leaders who create and mentor other leaders. I believe God is trying to take us to a place that is going to require multiple leadership, major leadership, exponential leadership.

**Chandler:** Where is God trying to take you next?

**Watson:** Not only are we called to be a regional church; we have a message for the nation and maybe a message for the world. I'm trying to make myself available for that. Part of our vision statement is that we are a "church for people on the grow, touching the world with love and communicating the positive power of Christ to our generation." That's what I'm trying to live out.

### Reflecting on the Trip: Questions for Continuing the Conversation

1. How do leaders move from a mode of "failure-avoidance" into visionary risk-taking?
2. If vision belongs to the congregation and is not simply "imported" by a pastor, in what ways can we create forums for conversation in which leadership communities imagine expansive ministry futures?

3. Spiritual leaders "exegete" cultures as well as sacred texts. How might a pastor learn, diagnose, and communicate a congregation's history in ways that empower them into preferred tomorrows?

4. How can leaders create or utilize "special days" (anniversaries, homecomings) or events (retreats, celebrations) to articulate new manifestations of God's vision for the congregation?

5. Where are the points at which pastors are most vulnerable to "losing their personhood" and "becoming their ministry?" What can pastors and congregations do preemptively to short-circuit these potential crashes?

6. If the teacher becomes a learner through teaching, what are the things we can do to develop potential and actual leaders around us in ways that will cause *us* to become better leaders?

## 9

*Interview with* **Erwin McManus**
Mosaic, Los Angeles, California
www.mosaic.org

# Courageous Diversity

Mosaic (formerly "The Church on Brady," "Bethel Baptist Church," and "The First Southern Baptist Church of East Los Angeles") currently meets in three locations in Los Angeles, California, including a nightclub. After a time of plateau and decline, the church has grown, reaching well over one thousand attenders each week. The church is widely recognized for its cultural diversity, utilization of the fine arts in worship and ministry, and its ability to reach a young, creative population in Los Angeles. Erwin McManus's background in philosophy and church planting informs the church's unrelenting pursuit of cultural transformation; the multicultural and artistic congregation gives the expression of this mission a beautiful and creative form.

**Here's a Trip-tik™ of things to watch for:**
✓ McManus's focus on the context-driven mission of the local church as part of the world mission of "The Church"
✓ Gracious acknowledgment and understanding of the role and influence of McManus's predecessor
✓ Imaginative language about the leader as cultural architect
✓ Prophetic language about the role of the "Pastor" and "pastors" and creative, artistic language about mission and calling
✓ The combination of heady conceptual, philosophical language and concrete advice about taking small, practical steps

✓ McManus's transparency about what has hurt him and why criticism has been difficult

✓ How McManus understands and practices classic church growth categories, but is careful to subsume descriptive sociology to imperative missiology and prescriptive theology

✓ Brutal frankness about the focus on the not-yet-Christian world, regardless of the demands of churched people

✓ Hope that transformational leadership happens through a series of short, attainable steps

---

**Chandler:** Tell us about the evolution of the church, as it has become "Mosaic."

**McManus:** The church is about seventy years old, maybe a little older. It has had several names. It was "Bethel Baptist Church." It was, legally, "The First Southern Baptist Church of East Los Angeles" for the longest period of time. Then it took on an identity called "The Church on Brady" (although legally it was still First Baptist of East L.A.). People began calling it, "The Church on Brady," so that became, in essence, the name. When I came in 1992 to The Church on Brady, it was a great congregation. It had a great history. It had a long-term pastor before me; Tom Wolf was its pastor for twenty-four years. He had been there for twenty years. He had done a great job of transitioning the church from a dominantly Caucasian congregation of people who had transplanted to California out of the South or Midwest. The congregation was, maybe, seventy-five people, and he grew the church to six hundred in attendance: a lot of families, blue-collar, Mexican American church with maybe 80 percent Mexican, 20 percent Caucasian.

**Chandler:** Was that a reflection of Tom Wolf's leadership, the neighborhood, the church's vision, or what?

**McManus:** The neighborhood was very much a blue-collar Mexican American community. He took a Caucasian transplant congregation and really moved them to reaching the community. It became very reflective of the community around the church. It was a wonderful community church in that sense. He had a great heart for missions, so the church drew (from other places) people who had a heart to go overseas, especially to the "10–40 Window."[1] And the church developed a reputation advocating for mission work around the world. They did a lot of work, early on, in Belize, and places like that. That's the upside. The challenges were also there. The

---

[1] The 10/40 Window is an area that contains the largest population of non-Christians in the world. It extends from 10 degrees to 40 degrees north of the equator, and stretches from North Africa across to China. For further information, see http://1040window.org.

church was at a plateau for fifteen years at about five hundred seventy-five in attendance. Then, for about four years, it began to decline. I can remember at one point we were dipping into the three hundreds. When you consider that the congregation had a high ratio of children per adult, we were into the two hundreds in terms of how many adults were actually attending. The congregation seemed to be unaware that they were declining, unaware that its economic health was unstable. At a certain point, we had nearly a million dollars in debt, a hundred thousand dollars budget deficit, and just over a thousand dollars in the bank.

**Chandler:** In other words, the dream church any new pastor would long to come to.

**McManus:** If you read a book about it, this might be considered a foolish thing for me to do!

**Chandler:** What was God saying that would draw you to become pastor in this place?

**McManus:** I didn't come to become pastor. I didn't come to come on staff. I came to Los Angeles because I had a real burden to be in L.A. and to try to reach the world from this spot. I had a real sense that L.A. was God's strategic city. My wife and I moved out here because we really felt called to Los Angeles, and to the world from Los Angeles. We felt this church was the right church to be part of, so I was just an attender. When I was in Dallas, Tom had asked me to consider being pastor, and without any hesitation, I said, "No!" I had no desire to be the pastor of this congregation. A year later, when we had moved out here, he talked to me again about being the pastor, and I said, "No." No desire whatsoever. My wife thought he was a great pastor and was happy for him to be the pastor and for me to be an attender. Really, "cognitive obedience" is the best way I can put it. I felt like God began to show me the needs in the congregation. Frankly, it wasn't that interesting to become the pastor when I was *outside* the congregation, because I felt like things were going pretty well. But when I came in and realized the church had been in fifteen years of plateau or decline, I then felt there was something important to do. As I got more involved with Tom and the congregation, the way I felt God had crafted me, the gifts that God had given me, and the experience God had put in my life were the right match with helping the church move into a new future. Honestly, I had no emotional desire to be pastor. It took several years for that to catch up with me.

**Chandler:** You behaved your way into believing.

**McManus:** I told my wife, "This is cognitive obedience. I feel that God is commanding me to become the pastor of this church." You know, a lot of guys want to be in charge; they want to be the leader. I can honestly say I was happy *not* to be. I really felt that God was giving me a responsibility, placing a burden in my heart. I stepped into what I felt was God's calling and command for my life.

**Chandler:** You don't describe yourself as "senior pastor," but as "cultural architect." Does that reflect your sense of call there, to what you feel God wants you to do and be as a leader?

**McManus:** Very much. I felt called to the transformation of Los Angeles, and to urban centers *through* Los Angeles. God placed me in the center of this community, and this community called Mosaic has a real calling to the transformation of the city. I think part of the problem is that many pastors feel called to their *churches* rather than to *cities with their churches*. I think we've somehow confused the sense of calling. When I look at the book of Acts, everybody seems to be called *out* rather than called *in*. Many times, pastors can't mobilize people outward because they (the pastors) were never called outward.

**Chandler:** The congregation follows the lead of the pastor, and if the pastor's attention is devoted to the machinations of the congregation, then the congregation itself follows that lead and turns inward.

**McManus:** Absolutely. Think about pastoral search committees. You look for a pastor who can meet your needs rather than a pastor who can reach a city. How many churches say, "It doesn't matter if a pastor fits *us*, it matters that a pastor fits this *community*. And we need to follow his leadership and become the kind of people that reach this community." Normally, we look for someone who will not disrupt the status quo, rather than someone who will come in and revolutionize the church to become what God desires the church to be. I keep saying, "I am not a very good pastor." We have great pastors in our congregation. We have people with unbelievable pastoral gifts. They're the people I want to unleash and empower, because they're the ones who will do the great work of pastoring.

**Chandler:** So your role as "cultural architect" is to equip the pastors rather than serve as "The Pastor."

**McManus:** To equip the pastors, to equip the teachers, to equip the evangelists, and to equip every believer in what they're uniquely called by God to do. I'm just not gifted enough to lead this congregation! I really believe that the gifts that are necessary to do what God wants here are encompassed in no one human being.

**Chandler:** In describing your own ministry and the call of your church to reach the city and the world, you've used the words "apostolic ethos." Tells us what you mean by that.

**McManus:** I am convinced that the church is the "Alka-Seltzer in the glass." The church is the agent that dissolves into the larger body and brings health or brings ingredients that bring health. The church is the key to the transformation of individuals, of families, of communities, of societies, of history. So "apostolic ethos" is talking about an environment created by healthy relationships to God and to one another, that engages the world in healthy relationships, and brings transformation. Many times, the whole idea of "pastors and teachers" has informed the ethos of our churches. But when you look at the book of Acts, "visionaries and dreamers" ignited the church. The prophecy Peter alludes to from the prophet Joel says that God is going to create a movement. This movement is going to be catalyzed by young men and old men having visions and dreams, and they will become servants and prophets. I look at the church and see that most of the time, the American church cannot be described as a movement of visionaries and dreamers. It is normally a movement of administrators and managers, or, at best, pastors and teachers. Many times, we actually squelch dreams and become the killers of visions, rather than the kind of community that catalyzes that environment.

**Chandler:** Mosaic reaches many artists. Is that a product of the neighborhood or city you're in, or is that a strategic component of helping this church become a "dreaming community"?

**McManus:** People are always saying, "It's because you're in L.A.," which is, by the way, a little bit irritating, for a variety of reasons. You can drive around L.A. and find an infinite number of churches that are squelchers of creativity rather than nurturers of creativity. At the same time, you can find incredible creativity all over the world. Now, L.A. may have a higher concentration of creativity, because many consciously creative people move here. But there isn't a church I know of anywhere in the world that doesn't sing. We all sing. Does that mean all those churches are located in Nashville? No, of course not. It's because we believe that music is a gift to the church and through the church, and that we worship God together through singing. It is amazing how many musical people we find in churches throughout the world. The reason churches do not have creative expressions is that they do not advocate creativity. We do not nurture it. Many times, we don't believe it exists in people. Many nations–in the Middle East, in North Africa–*squelch* that creativity because of a fear of unleashing the citizens of the country. Many times, I think what we see in totalitarian governments is what we also experience in local churches.

**Chandler:** What is envisioned by the name "Mosaic" in terms of creativity and in terms of the ministry you're called to do and the people you're called to reach? You reach a remarkably diverse group of people.

**McManus:** A church has to find a core identity and describe herself from that identity. Many times we get it by accident. Sometimes our denominational labels have become too important to us. When we're Baptist or Methodist or Presbyterian, we're communicating to other people that if you're *not* this, you're not a part of us. We wanted our central metaphor to be something that even a person who does not know God could connect to. We picked Mosaic. A "mosaic" is an art form, broken and fragmented pieces brought together by an artist to reflect the glory of God, especially when light shines though it.

**Chandler:** Kaleidoscope.

**McManus:** A kaleidoscope is a mosaic in motion. We wanted to say, "We're a community of broken and fragmented people, brought together by the masterful hand of God the artist to give him glory, especially when his light shines through us." One of the layers of that metaphor was to say, "Honestly, we're not perfect people. We're just broken and fragmented. We come to God *because* of our needs, not because we're perfect and have it all together." We also wanted it to be a reflection of the nations, saying that in Jesus Christ, the many become one. The wonderful thing about a mosaic is that it's more beautiful when the pieces are more dissimilar. Every piece isn't the same. They have all kinds of unusual shapes and designs. We wanted to say that the church isn't a place where you're cloned, you're standardized, and you're punched out from a mold. This is not assembly-line religion. Every person is unique, and God desires to accentuate that uniqueness through the redemptive power of Christ in your life.

**Chandler:** This is a sort of antithesis to the "homogeneous unit principle."

**McManus:** Well, we recognize this as a true sociological pattern; people tend to gravitate toward those who are like them. At the same time, just because you start some place doesn't mean you finish there. When we begin to advocate that gathering with "people just like us" is the appropriate and best way to gather, then I think we've then fallen short of God's heart. We want to say that you need to value people when they're different, because they're different. People can look like Jesus and not look like you!

**Chandler:** You study the homogenous unit principle, church growth, and the social sciences to understand the natural way people and groups flow. However, you don't allow this to be the final word in sculpting what the people of God are to look like in community.

**McManus:** I think you study social science or church growth, and ask yourself, "Is this descriptive, or prescriptive?" We need to be careful, because when something is being described as an observable reality, it doesn't mean it should be prescribed as the way God intends for it to be.

**Chandler:** Having listened to many of your sermon tapes, I've heard you say at times, "I'd rather reach one pagan in Los Angeles than get ten thousand people to go to church in Atlanta."

**McManus:** Now you're going to get me in trouble! [*laughing*] It's okay. I really mean it.

**Chandler:** Speak to the sentiment behind that statement.

**McManus:** Well, I know that there are a lot of people in Atlanta who don't know Christ, who need to be reached with the gospel. All I'm saying is that, many times, we have unintentionally created a competition that has the wrong goal. When we look at churches in terms of their size, how fast they're growing, all that sort of stuff, we rarely factor in where those churches are and who they're reaching. I just think that we ought to celebrate any church that is reaching anyone outside of the church culture. Anyone who genuinely has never heard the message of Christ, who is separated from Christ: agnostic, atheist, Hindu, Buddhist, or Muslim. I just love being in an environment where fewer and fewer people have a church background, and they're hearing the message of Christ in a fresh and new way.

**Chandler**: So you're interested in conversion growth, as opposed to swapping of church members, reactivating prodigals, and that sort of thing.

**McManus:** I know that it is important to reactivate people who have gone cold and fallen away. I think it's probably one of those areas God always has to speak into my life and say, "This is valuable." But it is certainly not a front burner issue for me. What is most important to me is to see people who have not yet had a face-to-face encounter with Jesus get that, and come to him.

**Chandler:** You're a forty-something pastor, yet your church has demonstrated a remarkable ability to reach twenty-something people, students, and singles. To what do you attribute this?

**McManus:** You're right; I'm forty-something. The average age of our church is mid-twenties. A good sixty percent of our church would be singles, ages eighteen to twenty-four or so. We're a pretty young congregation. I think a part of that doesn't have anything to do with age. Some of it is being able to speak in a meaningful way into the worldview, to the frameworks, and to the texture of the culture you're trying to reach. Frankly, a lot of the people we have in their twenties are looking for people who have lived life longer than they have, people who can make sense of the chaos and complexity of the world around them.

**Chandler:** They're looking for someone one step ahead, in front but within reach;–not two steps ahead, so far away that they can no longer connect.

**McManus:** Frankly, I think a person can be in their sixties or seventies. If they will strip themselves of the security of their own traditions and rituals, live an authentic life before God, and speak into the culture as it exists, they will have a huge hearing by anyone in their twenties.

**Chandler:** What do you do, as a follower of Jesus Christ, to ensure that you are accessible to people of a different generation?

**McManus:** We don't think generationally. I think the generational paradigms are far more Midwestern or Southern or East Coast kinds of frameworks. We really look at worldviews. What are the invisible assumptions from which a person organizes their reality? For me? It is just a relentless pursuit of truth; an unwillingness to hide behind cliché. Demanding yourself to look to the Scriptures for what they really say, even if they make you uncomfortable. I think those are the things that transcend generations.

**Chandler:** Can you give an example of how that played out in your life?

**McManus:** You have to remember, John, I didn't grow up in church. I didn't have to shake free of a lot of the assumptions of Christendom. My grandmother taught me about Jesus; my grandfather taught me about reincarnation. I was born into postmodernism. Many people see post-modern as a neat thing to be. If you grew up with those frameworks, it isn't so neat. I didn't have to discard a lot of churchy stuff, and the journey I came up on really helps me connect with people in the postmodern world. There have been people who have been thinking in a postmodern way for generations. It's not as if some of these frameworks are brand new. It's just that so many of our leaders and churches have never stepped into the real world and engaged in dialogue that is substantive. My son, when he was five years old, said, "Dad, Muslims believe in the Koran, and we say that the Koran isn't from God. How do we know that the Bible is not the same? We think it's from God. What makes us different from Muslims? How do we know?" Many parents have said, "Now, we just don't say that kind of thing. You're not allowed to ask those questions." We have to realize that if we can't answer those questions for our kids, we certainly can't answer them for people outside of our faith, outside of the influence of Christianity. We haven't had very good answers to very good questions. We've treated good questions as antagonism.

**Chandler:** What kinds of things continue to be difficult for you, as a believer and as a leader? And where have you found help in those things?

**McManus:** That's a good question. I tend to be optimistic, so that question doesn't come to me naturally. One of the things that tends to be difficult is that you live with endless criticism. I have yet to find a way to escape that. If anything, in the first twenty years of my Christian experience, I tried to do things where no one would criticize me, and would still be criticized all the time. Now that I've hit my forties, I've said, "All right, I've been terribly unsuccessful in making everybody happy; so now I need to focus on pleasing God." Doing what I know is right and letting the criticism come as it may. I think sometimes, as followers of Christ, we tend to be extraordinarily critical of people who are simply trying to follow God and usher in what God's doing in the generations. To this day, that's the hardest thing.

**Chandler:** What helps you get through that?

**McManus:** When Abraham Lincoln died, he had in his pockets some notes from people who had encouraged him. That tells me that people who have accomplished great things and are very successful are not saved from some of the same struggles that all of us have. What I try to do is talk to my wife. When she agrees with the criticism, I try to listen harder! When she agrees with it, I take a deep breath and say, "Okay, this is where you need to change." The criticism isn't there just to hurt you; it's there to help you. I try to take everyone's criticism and become a better person through it. I think some people criticize you because they love you and want to help you be more like Jesus. Yet some people criticize you because they want to hurt you. If I can take their criticism and grow from it, I have taken something that was intended perhaps even for evil, and allowed God to do the good he wants. The difficult thing about criticism is that it is almost always rooted in some level of reality. If my goal is to become more like Jesus, no criticism in the world can hurt me long term. In the end, I get to become more like Christ.

**Chandler:** When Jesus says, "Love your enemy," he means that your enemy has a gift for you that your friend can't give you.

**McManus:** That's right. Sometimes your friends won't tell you the truth.

**Chandler:** And you wish your enemies would quit.

**McManus:** Yeah! It's always easier to take it when it's motivated by love. But part of spiritual leadership is to learn from *everyone*.

**Chandler:** Many pastors and churches feel "stuck," even depressed. What word of hope could you say to folk who are stuck?

**McManus:** That is a more common condition that we would ever care to imagine. What I try to remind myself is not to worry about things I have no control over. I take responsibility for the things I can control. What I would say to leaders who are stuck is, sometimes we have huge dreams that are not matched with the convictions that will get us there. Sometimes what we need to realize is that small steps of faith, risk, and courage accomplish huge dreams. What I would say is very simple. I sat down with a man in my office and said, "What do you want to accomplish in your life?" He said, "I want to change the world." I said, "How are you going to begin?" He laughed and said, "That's the hard part." I said, "You will never change the world, because people who change the world change it one person at a time, one square foot at a time, one day at a time." What I know about every pastor or leader in America is that there is one person they can love; one person they can minister to; one person they can engage in a conversation; and one person they can help move to faith in Christ. If you can just start one person at a time, one step at a time, and one day at a time, at least you're moving toward that dream.

**Chandler:** "The kingdom of heaven is like leaven in a loaf" (Mt. 13:33, paraphrase).

**McManus:** Yes. Jesus also said that to the one who is faithful in small things, he'll give more. Sometimes we want "the more" and the small things seem too mundane.

### Reflecting on the Trip: Questions for Continuing the Conversation

1. Erwin McManus is transparent about his sense of calling, spiritual priorities, and ongoing difficulties. What does personal transparency cost church leaders, and how can it help as they lead?

2. More and more, pastors are being called from within congregations. How do we identify such prospective pastors? What are the challenges unique to exploring and accepting such a call?
3. How can church leaders model cultural and congregational inclusiveness while remaining evangelistic theologically?
4. Typically, pastors attract congregants who are approximately their own age, yet Mosaic's average attender is much younger than Erwin. What can we learn about how this might happen in other churches?
5. How can we help churches to move beyond focusing on their internal congregational culture and into redeeming the local culture around them?
6. How can a congregation's thinking and practices be enriched through utilizing categories of classical philosophy and the liberal and performing arts?
7. What can leaders do to help congregations think and act in terms of "city-reaching" rather that expending all of their energy on internal development and maintenance?

# 10

*Interview with* **Robert Cupp**
**Gary Harrell**
**Mickey Rapier**
Fellowship Bible Church of Northwest Arkansas, Lowell, Arkansas
www.fellowshipnwa.org

# Courageous Teamwork

One of several "Fellowship Bible" churches emanating from a mother church in Little Rock, Arkansas, Fellowship Bible Church of Northwest Arkansas is a nondenominational church of approximately six thousand weekly attenders. Robert Cupp, Gary Harrell, and Mickey Rapier serve as leaders. Absent titles, Robert's typical ministry responsibilities include catalytic and directional leadership and teaching; Gary mobilizes small group and lay ministry; Mickey leads the worship experience. Robert and Gary preach 15–20 weekends apiece in a typical year, with others teaching and preaching on other weekends. Their leadership model is intentionally based in counterpoint to a distasteful, ego-driven, "superstar pastor" model they have seen and found wanting.

**Here's a Trip-tik™ of things to watch for:**
✓ How to decide when it is better to start a new ministry than to reform an existing ministry
✓ Parlaying the blessing of a new facility into a setting in which people could more readily experience transformative hearings of the gospel
✓ Settings where lay leadership is not merely permitted but commanded

✓ Leadership when "no one is in charge"
✓ Working with other leaders who are like you, and different from you
✓ When to trade off the efficiency of Elmer's glue leadership for the long-term bonding of epoxy
✓ The core Kingdom values of team-based leadership

---

**Chandler**: "Why did God call Fellowship Bible into being, and how did that happen?

**Cupp**: God brought together seven families with a common desire to do church in a different way. In those days, although we didn't realize it, there was a vacuum for a unique style of ministry that was very strong in worship, family, and small groups. So these seven families found one another, banded together, and launched Fellowship.

**Chandler**: Nothing in an already-existing church scratched that itch?

**Cupp**: No. I was in a Southern Baptist setting as an associate pastor. As I looked down the road, I did not think I was going to fit well in the traditional Southern Baptist model. I didn't have an ax to grind. I wasn't caught up in theological controversy. I wanted to do things a different way; I wanted the freedom to try some new styles of ministry without tradition always saying no or "we've never done it that way before."

**Chandler**: You saw where Southern Baptists were heading, determined it to be a dead end, and said, "Let's explore a different way."

**Cupp**: It wasn't so much where they were heading but where they were. I was ministering in Northwest Arkansas in what was considered to be a very nontraditional Southern Baptist church. I wanted to move out of an associate role and into a "senior pastor" role (which was the only model we knew then), to do small groups instead of Sunday school, and to do some other things on the cutting edge. It didn't sound like, look like, or feel like Southern Baptist ministry. These other families had much the same feeling. We were from four or five denominational backgrounds. But we could all see something different. So that was the impetus.

**Chandler**: Where *did* you see glimpses of a new and different future?

**Harrell**: For me, it was in a parachurch model. I, too, had been raised in a Southern Baptist church. I wasn't comfortable with that. I didn't personally thrive under that model of ministry. It was not until I got into college that I found Christ outside of religion. I found Christ, and then through Christ, I was introduced to the model of Campus Crusade for Christ, and had a four or five year ministry in college and, later, on staff. There, I saw what I thought was a purer work of Christ, outside of the church. I'm still trying to answer the question, "How can we bring that model of ministry into the church?"

**Chandler**: You're asking, "How can a church catch a Spirit-filled, postdenominational experience of Christ?"

**Harrell**: You bet. How can a church do what it does not because, "That's the way we've always done it." How can a church take a fresh look at the New Testament Scriptures and try to be creative and innovative in reaching people for Christ, establishing them in the faith, and equipping them for ministry.

**Cupp:** The question was often asked, "Why can't you just go to a traditional Southern Baptist church, reform them, and be an agent of change?" However, the kinds of things we were thinking about in the mid-1980s were so far removed from the Southern Baptist way of doing things that it almost seemed unethical to go into an existing church with a treasured history and heritage, and change them into something that they were not. We were asking, "Is it right to do that?" Or would it be better to erase the marker board, start fresh, and just experiment and see what happens?

**Chandler**: At some point, you quit spending so much money on repairs and renovations, and start to build something brand new.

**Harrell**: Exactly. I think that was an impetus to success. Well, I'll call it "success;" we'll let the Lord judge that later. Let's say, the success of *this* church. We weren't fighting old battles, old wars. Once we started, we could honestly tell people who came to us with agendas, "That's just not who we are. That's not where we want to go. Please have the freedom to go. There are good churches in this area that might be a better fit for you." We'd recommend other churches out of concern for them, and out of concern for what we were trying to do here.

**Chandler**: After starting in 1984, how could you begin to tell you were hitting your stride with a new and different model of church?

**Cupp:** I'm realizing how hard it is now to think back that many years! Even back then, we were seeing life change, and were sensing the pleasure of God in what was going on. It's not that we didn't need a lot of improvement and development; we made a lot of beginner's mistakes in the early days. Yet there was a sense of excitement and enthusiasm that God was present, working, and that lives were being changed.

**Rapier**: Pretty rapid growth, too.

**Chandler**: What has the growth pattern been here?

**Cupp:** 15 to 25 percent per year for the history of the church.

**Chandler**: Steadily, or in spurts?

**Rapier**: We grew every year steadily. We had a pretty good spurt when we moved into the new building in 1991.

**Chandler**: So about halfway through the life of the church, you had a growth spurt that coincided with solving facility issues.

**Cupp:** Something interesting happens when you move from a junior high cafeteria, leave the smell of chilidogs, and go to your own place. In the culture's mindset, we were a *real* church when we had a facility. Even though that wasn't our thinking, I think that was the perception of the people who were now beginning to come in larger numbers.

**Chandler**: There were people waiting for you to build and move in before joining you.

**Rapier**: Apparently so. We were able to do things in our own building that we were only able to dream about in a cafeteria, such as dimming the lights, creating an experience which complements the theme and helps people walk out with something they can use. I think that was attractive to people. Based on Jim Pine's book *The Experience Economy* we hit on some of these ideas at a good time.

**Chandler**: Being able to move into the facility deepened your ability to lead people in an experience of worship and learning, the values incipient in the church. It wasn't just a place to park, and to park your child, but an enhancement of the core spiritual experience itself.

**Harrell**: Right. Earlier, your question was about when we hit our stride. For me it would be in the early 1990s. You get in the new building, you're doing three or four services, people are standing around the walls, and you sense that something is going on here! One thing was solid, stable, consistent leadership with a vision, an *evolving* vision. We also had great worship and celebration that used art to bring together all of the various dimensions of worship. Behind the scenes, a growing band of empowered believers were taking ownership for the ministry at a grass-roots basis.

**Chandler**: You had become an equipping church, where the ministry was done by the believers and not just by the pastors?

**Harrell**: Absolutely. It was incredible!

**Rapier**: It was about that time of getting the building that people would start to call and request, "Can my community group leader do the eulogy at my husband's funeral?" Or, "Can my community group leader baptize me?" Things like that, the whole mutual-shepherding aspect. They didn't have to have the hired guns to do that; they were looking to the community small group leaders to be the shepherds.

**Chandler**: You became a permission-giving church where people owned ministry, exercising spiritual gifts and taking care of each other rather than expecting staff to take care of them.

**Cupp**: Yes. Somewhere, we crossed the threshold of being simply a "permission-giving" ministry. It became a *mandate*, almost a compulsion, to find your ministry. How did God wire you uniquely in order that you might do ministry in a significant way? We left the "permission" side of it and moved to a "command" side of it. You *must* have a ministry and a mission, and get out there where real life is going on. Mix it up with the world.

**Chandler**: Fellowship Bible is noted for a "team leadership" model. Who's in charge?

**Rapier**: [*after a long pause, laughing*] Right now, you've got three monkeys covering their eyes, ears, and mouth! We were in front of the worship center one morning after services when a lady asks Robert across the way,

"Who is the senior pastor here?" I see him pointing to me and saying, "He is!"

**Harrell**: In my mind, there's no question that Robert is the directional leader, because he has the gifts of directional leadership. You drop him in any group, anywhere, and people would begin to gather around him, simply out of a basis of giftedness. Robert also looks to others for leadership in their own area. Our congregation is an organism. It's not just "head down," but the head processes input from the body. It's very organic.

**Cupp**: One of the unique things here is that, given the circumstance of ministry, any one of us three—or others who are not here—might be on the point. They might be, in a sense, the lead goose in a flock of geese. When necessary, they will fly to the front and actually lead us, taking responsibility for a particular area. My role is more directional and visionary and, especially, catalytic. I'm to enter into a situation and make something happen. We say, "Let's get something going." Then we'll decide, "Who should be on the point of this?" Right now, Mickey is on the point. He's an elder, Gary is an elder who has rotated off the board of elders, and I'm an elder. But Mickey's on the point right now. Not because he's an elder, or one of the pastors. He is the uniquely gifted guy who's got the passion and heart and vision to lead in a very specific leadership project. We're excited to follow him and his leadership. He's doing a great job.

**Chandler**: So your role, Robert, is to flush the flock of geese, and depending on where they need to go, someone will ride on the point of that?

**Cupp**: I think so.

**Rapier**: The thing that's unique about Robert is that he founded the church. He could have declared himself king from there on out. But number one, he doesn't want everything that happens here to reflect back toward him. His core value is: "A lot gets done when nobody cares who gets the credit." So you have a true team situation that's rare, because gifts of directional leadership often are matched with "gifts" of ego.

**Harrell**: Robert's quality of releasing ministers to lead empowers other ministers to do the same thing. If we were a team ministry in name only, not in reality, everybody would still be trying to do ministry in an old-wineskins way. We communicate a subtle message that we are a true team. Different people can take the lead at different points. Everyone is a leader at some level, because we are all influencers. We define leadership as "influence," setting the bar pretty low. So you can be a leader as a ten-year-old if you're influencing other ten-year-olds. Everybody can be a leader. Everyone is in the process of leading. Everyone has their *moment* for leadership. So, seize the moment!

**Chandler**: Leadership then is a matter of giftedness and calling, a sphere of relationships and influence, and a matter of belonging to a body of people who not only release you to lead in your season, but almost demand it.

**Harrell**: People who applaud you, encourage you, and support you with their own gifts. They correct and instruct. It's two-way between you and them.

**Chandler**: On a staff level, Robert was here from the beginning, 1984. Gary, you came in 1989, and Mickey in 1991. How did this team of leaders form, recalibrate, and gel when new leaders came on board the team? What issues surfaced as you incorporated new leaders?

**Cupp**: That's a good question.

**Rapier**: A lot of it emerged from relationships.

**Harrell**: We already knew one another.

**Cupp**: Gary and I had a prior relationship. I made it very clear to him and to his wife that, as the Lord led, I would like to co-labor with him. I have an incredible amount of respect for him and could not imagine working with someone I didn't *like*. I discovered in Gary a soul mate. We had similar interests and backgrounds. When Mickey came on board, something remarkable happened: the three-legged milk stool was complete, or perhaps the cord of three strands. He brought something into the relationship, Not only did he bring professional competency, a generous heart, a warm personality, and a wonderful family, but also a dynamic. Something clicked among Gary, Mickey, and me. It was never a jockeying for position, but it was like we were soul mates. Individually and corporately, we wanted something bigger and better than our "selves."

**Chandler**: Was it your similarities or differences that worked toward this richer picture?

**Cupp**: First similarities, then differences. I think we experienced what the textbooks write about: true synergy. The experience of the whole was much greater than the sum of the parts. That was true on an emotional level, a spiritual level, and a friendship level. We developed an incredible amount of trust, authenticity, openness, and even transparency. We had intimacy on a person-to-person basis. Yet, we had different gifts.

**Chandler**: You had to be different from one another so as not to be simply "sidekicks" who don't bring new accountability, strength, or synergy to the team.

**Cupp**: Yes.

**Chandler**: What has been uniquely difficult about having a true team model of leadership?

**Cupp**: It's not the most efficient way of getting things done. It is hard to forge consensus and to work through personal reservations for the sake of moving forward the team, whether there are three, five, or seven of us. Yet, in the long run, the payoff is better. The "unity of the Spirit in the bond of peace" (Eph. 4:3) is incredible on the back end of it. On the front end, it's very hard to make a leadership or a directional decision when everyone has a voice. You're trying to work through objections and concerns. It is a very inefficient way that still becomes incredibly effective in the long run.

**Chandler**: I see this image of the Elmer's glue, which bonds simply, cleanly, and almost instantly, versus epoxy glue, which is a mess to mix, resin and hardener...but which fuses things more tightly in the long run.

**Cupp**: Yes.

**Chandler**: How do you distinguish your team model of leadership from other church models of leadership that may be "team" in name only?

**Rapier**: You mean churches where everybody's a team, but the senior pastor's not on it? [*laughing*]

**Chandler**: Yes, the senior pastor's the coach, and everyone else has a uniform!

**Rapier**: Servant leadership. Robert and Gary are gifted leaders but also toilet scrubbers. We're all toilet scrubbers. There's no hierarchy. From the beginning, we all get down and dirty and do what needs to be done, no matter what.

**Harrell**: We use the criterion of having fun. Are we all having fun yet? Occasionally we ask each other that. One way to judge whether a true team exists is whether everybody is enjoying it. I think the level of healthy fun may be a marker of the level of "team" health.

**Chandler**: In a hierarchical model, whoever's on top is having fun, and the others who aren't on top are not?

**Harrell**: No, they're not having quite as much fun. It's a good point of self-evaluation. Am I still having fun here? Do we like doing what we're doing? Do we like doing it *together*? Are we a "band of brothers?" That's one measure for me.

**Cupp**: I think of a *Leadership Journal* cartoon I saw once, set in Egyptian times. There was a row of seven or eight slaves pulling a huge block for the pyramids. Sitting on top of the block was an Egyptian with a whip. The caption was him speaking to the slaves: "I want you all to know that, from the Pharaoh on down, we're all equally valued members of the team." That cartoon, for me, illustrates the kind of pseudo-team that has a strong, authoritarian, perhaps benevolent dictatorial leader. On staff, you feel like one of the slaves pulling the block. No amount of talk about "team" cuts it. What Mickey said earlier gets at the core of it: we all work equally hard, and we work together.

**Chandler**: Depending on where the big stone needs to go, sometimes any one of you is up there with the whip, and other times you're on the receiving end of the lash?

**Cupp**: Or maybe we just get off of the stone and get down there and pull. We don't worry about titles, pictures in the bulletin, whose name is in the paper, or who gets the pastor's parking spot. We're trying to labor together. We are a team who also happens to be a family.

**Chandler**: How and what does that teach the congregation? How do staff leaders relate to and interact with lay leaders?

**Harrell**: As "one with." I get to be involved with small groups ministry. Both Mickey and Robert are involved in that. I'm telling our small group leadership that they are leaders, believer-priests, and that God is calling them to a high calling. Be in the trenches with people, and I'll be with you, too. All of us are in there with the people. They lead community groups. We're all part of a community group. (At different times, we're leading or we're part of a group.) We're all involved in grass-roots ministries of evangelism, of building up the body, of care and counseling, and of equipping. Every person in staff is just "one of the people."

**Chandler**: Fellowship Bible employed this "team" model from the very beginning. You're a new church plant, and it's in your "D.N.A." Other existing churches, obviously, aren't wired that way. Yet they sense discontent: staff members feel over-utilized in ministry, doing it all and burning out; laypeople feel under-utilized and bored. Is it possible for such a church to transition toward a team-based model of leadership? Can existing churches be revitalized by moving to a team-based model of leadership?

**Cupp**: To me, there's nothing inherently wrong with some of the traditional approaches to ministry. If you're comfortable with it, if it fits the subculture in which you live, and if you're being effective in that arena, to change for change's sake would be a mistake. You have to understand who you are and where you want to go and what it will take to get where you want to go. I think there are some who are longing for a different kind of ministry structure. But you have to be convinced of a few things. You have to be convinced that the most important things are happening, not in the church office, with the staff, but out, as Gary says, in the trenches, where people live and work and play. You have to be convinced that the soldier on the front line is far more important than the so-called general back at the "command post" in the rear; that the people doing "life-on-life" ministry are the heroes. That your ministry will not be measured by your name in lights, or the size of your office, or extra perks. These things may be hindrances rather than helps. And that you want to build not only a team but a family. If you're into building consensus and mobilizing an army, then I'd say, "Great! Investigate team-based ministry, and what it would look like within your existing structure." But I would caution folks that it's much easier to build from scratch than to change something that has existed for years and years and years and has a lot of cultural baggage, and (no offense intended), a lot of denominational baggage as well.

**Chandler**: Is there a word of hope for those not called to be new church planters? What can an earnest pastor or staff person coming into an established, traditional, hierarchical-model church do to begin to reform toward a team model of leadership?

**Harrell**: I don't think you can come in and mandate "team" structure or ministry. It has to begin with the individual minister knowing his own heart. Does he personally embrace some of the core values Robert and Mickey have alluded to, such as servant leadership, shared ministry, empowerment, not caring who gets credit, and to be Kingdom-oriented? Having a mindset that you're into building the Kingdom and not your own church sends a message throughout the whole church and certainly to the staff. If a man has that heart, has those core values, and wants to partner with other men or women who share those core values, then I think the Lord will be very pleased with that. It reminds me of the Trinity itself, where there is unity in diversity. In the Trinity, there is give and care and share. Different persons move forward at different times to accomplish different purposes. I think the Lord looks on a church like that and says, "That looks like home to me. It feels like my essence there. I think I'll dwell there." I think God does dwell there in a special sort of way. So if a pastor has that vision, and just *lives and practices* it without having to declare it, the vision will permeate the congregation.

**Cupp**: Let me revisit one thing to what Gary has said. If I was thinking seriously about new paradigms of ministry, I'd read Greg Ogden's book *The New Reformation.*[1] If the premise of that book—mobilizing the laity for ministry—really strikes a chord in your heart, then that may be the best way to do ministry. Team-based ministry can be effective when you really don't care who is getting the credit. You're not gauging success by the "man at the top" because there *is* no man at the top. You're gauging success by what is happening out in the marketplace and in the neighborhoods. To embrace this, a compelling personal vision of empowering other people must drive you; a vision that wakes you up in the middle of the night. You have to believe that it's not "building my name, my church, or my little kingdom." The issue is, "How can we unleash the laity to do what God has always called them to do: to be salt and light in a watching and hurting world?" But if a person were not able to get some ego and personal issues out of the way and *embrace* team-based ministry, I would encourage such a person to stay with the senior leader, or the solo pastor model. To whatever degree is possible, practice giving ministry away to the people (laity).

**Chandler**: If the leader can begin with a personal experience of the Kingdom and be humbled by his or her own inability to live in that Kingdom alone, then that leader can begin to partner with others and begin to live out a team model. That would act as a mustard seed.

**Cupp**: It's not an easy thing to dethrone yourself from the pedestal: "Since I am a *senior* leader, everyone else must be a *junior* leader." It's not easy to place yourself in a position where you will gauge your personal success by how much ministry you can put into the hands of people, and

---

[1]Greg Ogden, *The New Reformation* (Grand Rapids: Zondervan, 1991).

see them succeed as they put ministry in the hands of other people, who then put ministry in the hands of other people. This is nothing more than a paraphrase of 2 Timothy 2:2, "teaching faithful people to teach other faithful people to teach other faithful people." It's not an easy way to do ministry. But our personal conviction is that it's the best way. It's the Kingdom way.

## Reflecting on the Trip: Questions for Continuing the Conversation

1. How does a leader reach the point of saying that reforming an existing ministry is too costly? When is beginning a new ministry an act of courage, not cowardice?
2. The criterion by which Fellowship staff measures "ministry success" is "life change." Is personal and communal transformation the standard by which you assess your ministry and congregation? If not, what is your standard?
3. Fellowship leaders are intentional and directive about creating atmosphere conducive to transformational experiences. How do pastors attend to experience "climates" in ways that are useful without being manipulative?
4. Team leadership without strong interpersonal goodwill is impossible. What early, concrete steps toward team-building can a staff with unsettled or undeveloped chemistry take?
5. If a leadership team is built first on similarities, and only then on differences, how might this insight impact a blueprint for gathering, building, or growing a staff?
6. What symbols (for instance, reserved parking spaces or titles) work counter to hopes for team-based leadership?
7. How can pastors and leaders help congregations evaluate effectiveness based on the "front lines" rather than the "command post," that is, by human and community transformation rather than church office efficiency?
8. Fellowship NWA understands that the model of the inner life and activity of the Triune God governs leadership. How can congregations and leaders articulate a vision, mission, and philosophy of ministry that is intentionally theological, grounded in the biblical text, and oriented toward the Kingdom?

# 11

*Interview with* **Steve Chang**
The Light Global Mission Church, Fairfax, Virginia
www.lgmc.org (in Korean)

# Courageous Vision

Steve Chang serves as founding and current pastor of The Light Global Mission Church. Between 1998 and the time of this interview, this Virginia Baptist congregation has grown to seven hundred adults in average weekly worship attendance (plus three hundred children and youth), and over one thousand attending every week in ten-member cell church groups. It has averaged 20 percent annual growth and has a twenty-year plan for sustaining that pace. Its leadership development and discipleship processes are as precise as one would expect from a student of physics and business (Chang's background). In 2004, the congregation purchased a thirty-three acre campus from a state power company and is working toward housing six language churches on that site, including Vietnamese, Latino, and Chinese congregations.

**Here's a Trip-tik™ of things to watch for:**
✓ The church's simultaneous Korean culture-consciousness and transcultural sense of mission and calling
✓ The impact of Chang's background in physics, business, software writing, and government work on his strategic thinking and pastoral leadership
✓ The blurred lines between lay and pastoral leadership
✓ Steady, sustainable, planned growth that is part of a projected twenty-year plan and is surprising to no one in the church

✓ A highly evangelistic church whose sense of ministry is heavily humanitarian;

✓ A poetic description of the relationship between fear and faith for the courageous leader

---

**Chandler:** How did The Light Global Mission Church come into being in 1998?

**Chang:** Light Global Mission Church was started as a branch church of the Global Mission Church of Greater Washington, which is located in Silver Spring, Maryland. There were a number of people going to GMC from Virginia, and the leadership felt people were driving too much, so they spun off a Virginia congregation. After several months of preparation and prayer, we started this satellite ministry.

**Chandler:** Were you mentored at GMC to become a pastor for this branch church?

**Chang:** Yes. After one and a half years of satellite status, we started formally in March of 1998. In 2000, another Korean American Baptist church in serious financial trouble approached us to merge congregations. At the time, they had fifteen or so members and a two million dollar mortgage. At the time, we had about one hundred and fifty members.

**Chandler:** How long before the ministry here began to find momentum and grow?

**Chang:** We have averaged 20 percent growth annually except for two or three years.

**Chandler:** How long do you think the church can sustain twenty percent growth?

**Chang:** When we started, I laid out a twenty-year vision for the church. I had a very reasonable faith that it will be that way.

**Chandler:** A ministry plan of twenty years of 20 percent annual growth? [*Chang nods.*] That would be a remarkable story in North American Christianity!

**Chang:** [*nodding and laughing*] Reasonable faith.

**Chandler:** This is your first pastorate. How did your experiences as a physics student, businessman, software writer, and government servant impact your pastoral leadership?

**Chang:** The most important thing is that I can understand my congregation much better. I seldom preach at other churches. One time, I was preaching on a Wednesday at a New Jersey church. They asked me to speak on Sunday for a revival and I turned them down. Four of the elders came to see me after the service and asked me to come back to do a full revival. I said, "I don't usually do that. Is there some reason you are insisting?" Then one of the elders told me, "You are the first preacher we can immediately sense that, 'This guy understands us.'" That may be one of the most precious compliments anyone has ever given me as a Christian and leader.

**Chandler:** How were you trained as a leader? I know there was seminary work; did that come later?

**Chang:** I was raised in a pastor's family, with the expectation from my parents that their only son would one day be a pastor. When I received Jesus Christ as my Savior as a sophomore in college (even as a pastor's kid!), I immediately began witnessing, discipleship training, and learning from my friends and colleagues. I quickly realized, "I don't really have to be a pastor to be a good Christian minister." I had been working as a lay minister for ten years. Though my study of physics and my business were demanding, I was spending even more time in my church ministry. I realized at some point that I could only do one really well. I started to pray, and somehow God showed me several very clear signs that I should go into pastoral ministry full time. I had lots of pastoral training and experiences as a lay leader. I would even say that 90 percent of what I am doing right now as a pastoral leader is identical to what I did as a lay leader. I do now the same things I used to do.

**Chandler:** Just because you're the lead pastor doesn't mean you are functionally different than when you were a lay leader.

**Chang:** They have been fundamentally the same, 10 percent difference in the chief leader role.

**Chandler:** What falls within that 10 percent difference? What sorts of things are involved in your role as lead pastor that were not part of lay ministry?

**Chang:** Even in lay ministry, I did a lot of vision casting, because I set up all sorts of mission organizations. As this church grew past the one hundred and fifty barrier, I had to spend more time on operational management. I had been finding vision and transferring the vision to congregational leaders as a lay minister. But in the "body church" leadership (as opposed to the "cell church" level), certainly I had to spend time in managing staff, running day-to-day operations, and that kind of thing. That was the 10 percent of new stuff.

**Chandler:** You mentioned casting vision. This church has a remarkable vision of hosting multiple ministries or congregations on a single campus, with a stand-alone youth and children ministry. Can you describe this vision for ministry?

**Chang:** When we started the church, I tried to find out what kind of church was needed in this area. I found out that the Korean community in this area is only about 3 percent of the total population. We are working in a population that will limit our growth if we only focus on reaching Korean people. What will be our strategy if we want to sustain measurable ministry growth in this area? Naturally, it came to me that, as we grow larger, we were going to spend more time in helping other churches. I just realized that we as Koreans needed to minister to our neighbors.

**Chandler:** So the church began with a vision of reaching Fairfax, and not just Koreans in Fairfax?

**Chang:** Yes.

**Chandler:** If Koreans are only 3 percent of Fairfax, then we'll have to reach other people groups as well in order to reach the entire area?

**Chang:** Yes, that's right. So we are not going to be able to reach the other people groups by having them become Korean. The best way is to reach them is in their own language. Suddenly, this opportunity of a large parcel of land and buildings came to us, and we just naturally proceeded.

**Chandler:** So this campus is to be composed of multiple ethnic groups, each speaking their own language, rather than a single conglomeration speaking Korean or English; why is that?

**Chang:** Well, this is my personal belief: the ideal congregation in this world is just not a single congregation of different colors and languages thrown in together, in one place. Church consists of family units and not just individuals. Families are more deeply rooted in their cultural and ethnic backgrounds. I believe that it is more efficient to have the different ethnic congregations on one campus, together on one site but with reasonable fences. The way I see the campus is that each of the six or so congregations has their own space, but each congregation's children and youth would meet together in a common space. I pay a lot of attention to this in a campus of ethnic congregations. For most ethnic congregations, their most serious difficulty is children and youth ministry, mainly because of the language problems.

**Chandler:** Because the children and youth are second- or third-generation immigrants and are primarily English speakers, as opposed to their first-generation immigrant parents?

**Chang:** Yes. Ethnic congregations usually don't have enough pool of English-speaking teachers to put together a distinct, primarily English-speaking youth or children's ministry. Even children of different language backgrounds can be quite similar culturally. Their "youth" identity is often more pronounced than their ethnic identity.

**Chandler:** So you're treating "children and youth" as discrete people groups, regardless of ethnicity?

**Chang:** Yes. English-speaking second- and third-generation immigrants across ethnic groups may have more in common with each other culturally than they do with first-generation people of their own ethnic group. So we are developing a youth and children's ministry that will eventually become a separate religious corporation, almost like a parachurch organization, with their own budget. Then other ethnic churches can use this centralized ministry and pay a charge, say fifty dollars. That way, they don't have to spend so much money starting a children's ministry from scratch. This will help them focus on their adult ministry. Even the facility needs should be halved if you don't need specific space for children and youth ministry.

**Chandler:** By having these high-demand needs taken care of efficiently, each ethnic group can focus its resources more strategically.

**Chang:** Yes. Actually, I think the churches will be much better off not having to provide distinct and expensive space.

**Chandler:** Many churches that have grown like the Light Global Mission tend to expend most or all of their attention and energy on their own local ministry. Yet your church has adopted churches in South Carolina and Texas as branch churches, providing pastors and leaders, and also seems to have a strong national and international ministry. What is "Global" about this church?

**Chang:** There are about two dozen "Global Mission Churches" world-wide, from Uzbekistan, Canada, Korea, Australia, to New Zealand. It is a loosely connected fellowship. From the beginning, the Global Mission Church has emphasized world mission. We are also a "world" church.

**Chandler:** In what sense?

**Chang:** Not just global in a geographical sense. We have a heavy emphasis on nontraditional missions, non-"faith-based" missions, and humanitarian missions. We have a very close relationship with groups like "Interaction," a very large association advocating international humanitarian assistance. I serve on their board of directors. This mission is lobbying the United States government and the United Nations for international assistance; also the World Bank, International Monetary Fund, and other international bodies. We work very closely with a Korean American body that specializes in humanitarian aid in North Korea, as well as a couple of other human rights groups. We're "global" not just geographically, but across the spectrum of treating human need. Even in sensitive areas like North Korea.

**Chandler:** So "global" can mean advocating for human rights and humanitarian needs as well as pertaining to world evangelization?

**Chang:** Sure.

**Chandler:** Where is courage required for you as a leader, and for this church?

**Chang:** [*long pause*] The most significant signs of growth that I have ever seen in my congregation, not just in a quantitative but also in a quali-tative sense, relate to the organizational learning process as we grew. We had several opportunities really testing our faith, making hard congrega-tional decisions. People are always hesitant and doubtful. But as we went past one faith experience after another, I watched my congregation grow accustomed to making radical faith decisions. That is, I think, the most blessed experience we had. As a leader, I had to show my own faith at each of those faith decisions.

**Chandler:** Model the way.

**Chang:** Right. I had to stand there and go through it with them. My personal definition of vision is that you lead the people to the place where you haven't been before yourself. If you go to the place where you personally have been before, then you are a guide or a sherpa, but not a leader. Each time my congregation had to make a faith decision, it is also the same faith decision for me personally. I have no idea of what's ahead! I haven't seen it; I haven't been there; this is new territory; this is uncharted territory for me. But I have to show my confidence and faith in the Lord. I also have to show my people that they can trust God by showing how I trust God. When I turn around and face my people, I don't show nervousness. I show a face of calm. But when I turn around and face the direction we are heading, it can be despairing or terrifying. Those are the kinds of moments when the leader needs courage the most. In these first few years, we've been through quite a few of them. As we pass those times of faith decisions, people build more faith in the Lord. They also find faith in the leader. If you will walk them through those, after quite a number of those experiences, they are apt to believe almost anything you say [*laughing*].

**Chandler:** The courageous leader is both confident and fearful.

**Chang:** The sculptor who carved Lincoln's statue in the Lincoln Memorial intentionally did the design and lighting in such a way that his left face is dark and his right face is very bright. His left face is muscled and right face is gaunt. He intentionally wanted to show that Lincoln had two faces. When Lincoln was once accused of being two-faced, he once joked, "If I had two faces, would I wear *this* one?"[1] But he did have two faces.

**Chandler:** The courageous leader is two-faced.

**Chang:** I am fatherly to my congregation and terrified before the Lord. Two faces. The leader is the one who stands on the line, who stands before the completely unknown, and yet has to provide comfort and assurance for the people, as if in a home. For me, it is like an hourly flip-flop. I go back and forth several times within a day. The courageous leader is the one who is willing to live with that.

### Reflecting on the Trip: Questions for Provoking and Exploring

1. What is included in the 10 percent of things that distinguish the point leader from other leaders?
2. If we are convinced that God wastes nothing, how can we bring the insights gleaned from our familial, educational, and vocational experiences to bear on our congregational leadership?
3. Many churches are surprised by unforeseen growth and learn about its causes retroactively. Can a congregation follow the lead of the Light

---

[1]This story appears in several Web sites. See, for example, the newsletter of the *Farmington Community Library*, http://www.farmlib.org/mrrt/0105.pdf, page 2.

Global Mission Church and develop a plan on intentional, incremental, steady, and sustainable growth?

4. How can different groups within a church (or between churches) maintain an independent sense of identity while remaining interdependent in shared ministry?

5. Are there ministries your church could undertake that would serve other area congregations? Why is this rare?

6. The "guide" or "sherpa" role within a group is a safer, more familiar, and more comfortable role than being a leader who is "co-terrified" with the congregation. Where are places that you need personally to grow in your own faith in order to ask others to grow along with you?

7. What are the mistakes of the one-faced leader? Which is the more difficult leadership "face" for most of the leaders you know: the terrified face of the leader facing the unknown, or the comforting face with which the leader addresses others who are frightened? Which is more difficult for you?

# 12

# What We Are Learning from
# These Leaders (So Far!)

*How do insights from this diverse body of courageous leaders inform our hopes of transformational ministry? What are some of the broad-based "take-aways" that will inform our leadership practices? How do their struggles and triumphs inform our stories?*

We promised in chapter 1 to circle back after the conversations and gather learning about *vision, leadership,* and *structure.* Specifically, we were looking for insights on such issues as how leaders:

- Maintain *clarity* among the clutter of competing visions
- Exhibit courageous, rigorous *honesty* in congregations
- Persist in opportune *reinforcement* of vision and values
- Filter *criticism* appropriately
- Attain sufficient *tenure* for long-term effectiveness
- Find life-giving *learning communities* and opportunities
- Learn when, what, and how to *release* ministry
- Shed favored habits and customary practices when evolving situations dictate
- Thrive in ever-growing complexity

What are we learning about courageous church leadership from these practitioners?

## About Vision: Maintaining Clarity, Courageous Honesty, and Opportune Reinforcement

### *Clarity*

*1. Often, the obstacle to vision clarity is within the leader.*

Perhaps leadership courage begins with internal courage in naming the powers that haunt you as a leader–whether a "performance trap," or "approval addiction." David Chadwick describes a deadly cocktail: mixing his codependency as a people-pleaser with the popular notion that a church member's spiritual status or well-being could be based on a personal relationship with the pastor. Lance Watson and others describe a level of personal brokenness that they later deemed painful but necessary. They had to hit bottom in order to recalibrate their vision of ministry and their proper role in it.

*2. The ultimate measure of Kingdom vision is human and community transformation. Congregational transformation is but a means to that greater end.*

Chadwick and Leith Anderson remind us that it is not the pastor or the church's style that should unite the church, but the church's vision and values. Michael Slaughter suggests that we become what we measure, and that leadership is a matter of changing what we measure. For him it is not attendance, buildings, and cash, but whether we are creating revolutionary followers impacting communities in revolutionary ways. Brian McLaren suggests that once the church "got the walls built," the leadership task was to shift the core question to one of how the church could now get people to live out their faith beyond the walls. Erwin McManus is intentional about the church's language, particularly his title. He is not "senior pastor" but "cultural architect," because the end game at Mosaic is not to lead the church to grow, but to change Los Angeles and the world with the gospel. The goal is not to meet the needs of the church but to transform the city. Steve Chang is not content to let his congregation cloister in a Korean subculture; his desire is to transform his local and global communities, which requires a terrifying faith and great cultural flexibility.

### *Honesty*

*1. Admission of personal defects to oneself and others is the pathway to the next level of leadership.*

For Chadwick, the possibility of leaving Forest Hill for another church spurred a crisis of personal honesty that the transfer growth of his church was personality-driven and unsustainable. In Watson's case, it took the forced quiet and stillness of a long airplane ride in the middle of a frenzied ministry to unearth the painful self-admission: "I had become my ministry." Only then could he begin rebuilding his broken inner world. Many of these leaders describe dark nights or cold winter seasons of the soul. Often these were times when they could no longer mask insecurities, sins, or "issues." Chang admits to an almost-daily requirement to stand before the terrifyingly unknown frontiers of his own needs to grow in faith.

*2. Frank and ongoing assessment of one's giftedness and calling are critical matters of open discussion.*

Fred Craddock shares that an honest self-assessment of his gifts led to the conclusion that those gifts were no longer a match for what the church needed once it reached a certain size. That is the factor that helped him know it was time to leave. He wishes for more open and nonthreatening forums in which these conversations can happen in congregations. Happy would be the congregation and leader who were able to diagnose and discuss "a season, and a time for every matter under the sun" (Eccl. 3:1).

*3. Sometimes we are compelled to announce that "the emperor has no clothes."*

Slaughter reminds us of the prophetic calling to tell people in church the painful truth that followers of Jesus are not consumers or customers, but missionaries. McLaren articulates the frustrating reality of when Cedar Ridge's in-grown community no longer reflected their evangelistic vision, and he called for a full, radical reboot of the church (complete with planned death and resurrection). These are neither fun nor happy messages, but courageous and necessary ones.

### Reinforcement

*1. Persistent repetition of the vision is irreplaceable.*

Watson says that Nehemiah teaches that people have to be reminded of the vision every twenty-six days or they lose it. His most important task is to invest in the leadership of others. This investment is about embedding and reinforcing the D.N.A. of the vision in leaders. Chadwick describes intentional processes (new members classes) for setting expectations from the start of any new person's relationship with the church. The only way out of a ministry that is steered solely by meeting the expectations of others is to set expectations early and often. These expectations are grounded not in an authoritarian desire to dominate, but in the vision and values of the church.

*2. Articulate interpretation and daily incarnation of vision are ongoing mandates.*

Anderson says, "We are rigorous in avoiding church jargon, making sure people don't have to break a code to know what we're talking about." As a sociologist, he reminds us of the harmful effects of creating "in-group/out-group" barriers through inappropriate use of shorthand language.

Chang expands the clearly evangelistic commission of the congregation to include advocacy for human rights and humanitarian aid locally (for people groups other than his own) and globally.

McManus reminds us that vision is not something we simply preach about, but something we incarnate. Threatened by the enormity of a

God-sized vision, every leader still has one person they can serve, one thing they can do, one word to share Christ, and one person they can love. It is never wrong to do those right Kingdom things. They participate in and point to the larger Kingdom vision of which they are a part.

## About Leadership: Processing Criticism, Gaining Tenure, and Finding Life-giving Learning Communities

### Criticism

*1. Criticism of leaders by congregations is a pervasive and painful thorn in the flesh.*

Slaughter reflects that even though "cross" and not "ladder" is the metaphor for the Kingdom of God, he has felt so beaten up by streams of "Pastor Pigface" letters that he has been tempted to "climb the ladder" and leave. McManus confesses that the hardest thing he has had to deal with in ministry is relentless criticism. His only way to redeem it is to make a commitment to learn from everyone, including his critics and enemies.

Interestingly, both of these leaders are widely (and rightly) perceived as fearless and prophetic. They both reflect on the meaning of criticism. Yet, like Elijah immediately after confronting the prophets of Baal, they share moments of terrifying vulnerability. (See 1 Kings 19:2.)

I find this "culture of criticism" to be epidemic in churches. It is more distracting and damaging to pastors—and perhaps especially their relatives—than many might imagine. Could this be a major factor in the crisis of emerging leadership for North American churches?

*2. Leaders can and should quarantine destructive criticism.*

Chadwick frankly claims that "closing the back door is overrated." Some critics may need to leave the church in order for that church to move fully into God's mission for it. Author Peter Wagner has frequently shared the indelicate observation that some churches are about three funerals away from growing! Chadwick and Slaughter recall that as painful as it was to say goodbye to some church members after conflict, it was no net loss to the Kingdom. It was a necessary pruning for their churches to move forward.

In my own pastoral leadership, I experienced the harm of a persistent critic, "Ed." This is not to suggest that my leadership was above criticism; it was not. Nor is it to claim that all of Ed's points were invalid. (Note: a blind squirrel sometimes finds an acorn, a stopped clock is right twice a day, and occasionally what Ed had to say was trenchant.) Over a span of ten years, I kept a file of venomous letters from Ed and put out countless fires started on the platform of his Sunday school podium and in leadership meetings. One day, Ed determined that he would not win, and left our congregation for another church. Within six months of his departure, after a long plateau, our congregation grew by 40 percent and reached new heights of evangelistic effectiveness. Can I prove a connection? I wish I had pressed for Ed's exit much earlier, and I wonder what opportunities we missed because I did not.

Anderson puts it this way: "We do not reward dysfunction. We deal with critics one-on-one, quickly," thus not allowing them to spread poison in public forums.

Filtering criticism is the inescapable work of a leader. It is fun to be with uncritical lovers. It is difficult to process the painful truths of a loving critic. It is mandatory to deal decisively with a persistent and unloving critic.

### Tenure

*1. There is a strong correlation between effective, courageous ministry and a long-term match of pastor and congregation.*

With the exceptions of Craddock and Chang, every pastor interviewed has served for over fifteen years; some for over three decades. Many intend their current ministry to be a lifelong vocation. Slaughter notes that it took serving for a decade or two to find his "sweet spot" in effective leadership. From the beginning, Chang set out a twenty-year ministry plan.

*2. Long tenure is a joint project between pastor and people.*

Anderson's board unanimously discerned that he was God's leader for the church, and publicly resolved to affirm that leadership no matter the forthcoming opposition to leadership initiatives. That up-front resolution was indispensable toward a long, effective tenure.

*3. Succession planning will be critical.*

What happens after long-tenured leaders leave? Succession planning may be the central issue for complex churches led by founding or long-term pastors. Bob Russell describes letting go of long-held leadership roles, including the role of being the exclusive voice in the pulpit; this releasing is part of intentional succession planning.

Perhaps the Fellowship Bible staff points us toward the most sustainable solution to succession issues. For them, the longevity of any one person's leadership is based on the fact that none of them cares who gets the credit. They say, "We don't gauge things by "the man at the top" because there is no "man at the top." Their team-based leadership may pave the way for the entry of future leaders into the leadership community. Robert Cupp, as founding pastor, could have declared himself king. But in choosing to form and participate in a leadership community instead, he is unleashing a congregation where every believer is commanded to lead out of their giftedness.

### Learning Communities

*1. There is a horizontal revolution happening!*

Fellowship Bible staff are most articulate about intentional leader to learner, peer to peer, and mentor to protégé networks. They intentionally focus on scouting, coaching, and connecting emerging leaders. Slaughter ties Ginghamsburg's turning point to the creation of a revolutionary community of Joshuas and Deborahs that embodied the Kingdom dream they were called to become. To them, the leader is only the leader when participating in such a community, and in it, empowering others to lead. Leading is never about title or position, only gifts and fruit.

Moreover, there is much fruit in connecting with and learning from leadership communities outside of your own congregation. Anderson suggests that the best way to facilitate change in a church is to find another congregation at the next level and have your leadership community learn from theirs. The true horizontal revolution will be in full gear once intrachurch learning communities mushroom into interchurch learning communities. We are beginning to see signs of this in North America. May the movement grow!

*2. Learning communities keep leadership dialogical, energizing, and accountable.*

Craddock addresses leadership through the lens of preaching: if it is all one-way, then it is a bully pulpit. Courageous leadership means ensuring that the leadership is a product of true dialogue. This dialogue is more than an opportunity for the leader to disseminate already-decided-upon information; that is promotion. Courageous leaders are willing to have their minds and hearts changed by other leaders. McLaren speaks of honoring other leaders in the church by letting them have input, and coming to them with questions, and not just answers. Chadwick recognizes that only when he understood that learning was a two-way enterprise was he granted a new level of leadership authority.

McLaren points to how the community keeps individuals accountable. It is the community of faith, in a triangle with the Holy Spirit at one point and Scripture at the other, that helps us discern the will of God. The word *idiot* has its origins in the picture of a person who tried to live outside of the village.[1] The most dangerous leaders are the ones with the most credibility. Long-tenured, beloved leaders are most in need of the accountability that comes from being but one voice in a larger leadership community.

*3. These communities are a source of energy, strength, and joy to those in them.*

Anderson speaks of staff and board meetings that are invigorating, collaborative, synergistic, laity-empowering leadership communities. Why would anyone return from vacation to be a part of such a meeting? The answer is that one does so when finding those places to be challenging, affirming, and stimulating to better Kingdom living and ministry.

### About Structure: Releasing Ministry, Shedding Outdated Practices, and Thriving amidst Complexity

#### *Releasing*

*1. Pastors in growing ministries understand and practice appropriate "span of care."*

---

[1] See the article titled "Village Idiot" in *Wikipedia*, the online encyclopedia, http://en.wikipedia.org/wiki/Village_idiot.

Slaughter learned early that one pastor cannot give "institutional (pastoral) care" to more than ninety people. He concludes that unless leaders believe reaching ninety people is the final and full Kingdom potential of their churches, they must practice a different ministry model. Russell frames the issue by remembering that sometimes the only way to feed an entire congregation is to stop pleasing individual requests. He traces the pull toward pleasing individuals to the sometimes co-dependent need to be thought well of—a form of addiction to the approval of others. Courageous leaders still engage in life-on-life ministry. But instead of doing so in a random, emergency-based way, they intentionally pour their personal energies into others toward the end of reproducing and multiplying ministry.

2. *The way beyond hoarding ministry is to measure outcomes of transformation.*

Chadwick argues that the picture of a full-functioning "body of Christ" supersedes the "shepherd-sheep" model. Fellowship Bible staff gauges effectiveness by how much ministry is put in the hands of other people. It is not about "how much ministry I do"; it is about how much ministry is done through the ministers I equip to do the ministry. Here is the clear, biblical role of the pastor "to equip the saints for the work of ministry, for building up the body of Christ" (Eph. 4:13).

The measure of ministry does not lie in the personal comfort satisfaction within the minister doing the ministry, nor in the reputation gained among others for doing so. Ministry effectiveness is ultimately judged by how much life change occurs in people. How do leaders grow by doing this ministry? How does this ministry, transformed through the power of God, touch the people?

### Shedding

1. *Courageous leaders create congregational cultures where change is assumed, transition is welcomed, and leaning into the future is the default posture.*

McLaren's compelling arguments about not fussing over little changes are based in the idea that a congregation's attitude toward change itself is of major importance. For some congregations, the only good change involves a wet diaper. Others say, "If we don't like change, we'll like irrelevance even less." An effective leader can help frame change as opportunity, something to be embraced, learned from, and a tool for growth. McLaren suggests that we do not want to frustrate innovators who may offer great contributions if not bogged down by a congregation that argues over every jot and tittle.

Often congregational changes relate to cultural shifts, not to doctrine or belief. McLaren speaks of intentionally removing non-gospel barriers to people entering a community of faith. Some barriers addressed were as superficial as clothing style; others were more involved, like the tacit expectation that church attenders would share a common political affiliation or philosophy. The belief that their mission field was evolving drove much of his church's wrestling with shedding customary practices and rituals. They had to release some "old economy" attitudes in order to connect with postmodern seekers.

The way Anderson says it is, "We make sure the past gets a vote, but not the only vote. The future must also get a vote."

*2. There are strong cases to be made for both evolutionary and revolutionary strategies for spurring change and transition in congregations.*

The guiding proverbs of some of our interviewed practitioners might be, "Cry only once!" or "Whoever hesitates is lost." For others, though, the proverbs would be, "Measure twice, cut once," or, "Look before you leap."

McLaren places more hope in radical change ("maximized discontinuity") than incremental change. The latter, even when successful, tends to reward a change-averse mentality and to demoralize innovators. The Fellowship Bible staff even determined that it would be unethical to try to reform an existing church with the overwhelming changes required by their envisioned model of ministry. They argue that it is easier to build from scratch than to reform something that has existed with baggage for years and years.

On the other hand, Russell says that sometimes steady pressure toward incremental change over the long haul is called for. He leads the church to make changes "slowly, one-by-one, and with excellence." Anderson echoes this philosophy, noting that Wooddale's growth has been evolutionary rather than revolutionary. The chief benefit of this adaptive growth has been its durability or sustainability. Based on this outcome, Anderson claims that most churches should change incrementally.

So which proverbs are true? In Old Testament Wisdom writings, the proverbs were offered as a way of dealing with life situations not covered directly by Torah commandments. Wisdom was an aid to help us replicate the patterns of heaven. Sometimes that meant, "Do not answer fools according to their folly, / or you will be a fool yourself" (Prov. 26:4). Other times it meant, "Answer fools according to their folly, / or they will be wise in their own eyes" (Prov. 26:5).

So do we answer the fool or not? Well, that depends on what is appropriate and fitting in the unique circumstance. Some congregations need to be led into radically discontinuous change strategies; others need only gentle, sustained guidance. Some need resurrection, others only renewal. Effective practitioners match the change and transition strategies with the unique circumstances of the congregation.

### Complexity

*1. There can be great blessings in spiraling complexity.*

Certainly there is an undesirable type of complexity that is the product of entropy and hypercontrol. It is no badge of honor to "make things harder than they need to be." Too many churches have convoluted and overly complicated systems of decision-making that make forward movement difficult or impossible.

However, complexity can also be a byproduct of expanding ministries that demand higher levels of comprehensive, systemic thoughtfulness. Russell counters the common perception that larger churches lose spiritual vitality and connection. Southeast Christian experienced measurably better discipleship benchmarks in the face of increased complexity. For Watson, Saint Paul's growth from a "7-11 to a regional mall, with anchors and specialty stores" was not only an indicator of its increased complexity, but also of its greater faithfulness to its Kingdom calling and potential.

*2. Leadership amidst complexity requires humble, patient sharing.*

There can be joy in the humility of understanding that any one individual cannot be the conduit through which the whole of God's ministry in a congregation should flow. McManus said, "I am just not gifted enough to do what this church is called to do. So I have to equip a wide variety of gifted people to carry out that calling." It is sometimes easier to "just do it myself." But this is often an abrogation of the core leadership task to identify, equip, and deploy other leaders for Kingdom ministry.

Fellowship Bible's staff confesses that this form of leadership is sometimes slow, messy, inefficient, and complex. But once it bonds, its bond is stronger. In the same way, leaders who take the time to navigate complex systems in complicated churches, and who are patient to share leadership, will be rewarded with Kingdom outcomes much more profound than those produced by any individual.

## Summary

Here, then, is a summary of what we have been learning so far from these effective practitioners about vision, leadership, structure:

1. Often, the obstacle to vision clarity is within the leader.
2. The ultimate measure of Kingdom vision is human and community transformation. Congregational transformation is but a means to that greater end.
3. Admission of personal defects to oneself and others is the pathway to the next level of leadership.
4. Frank and ongoing assessment of one's giftedness and calling are critical matters of open discussion.
5. Sometimes we are compelled to announce that "the emperor has no clothes."
6. Persistent repetition of the vision is irreplaceable.
7. Articulate interpretation and daily incarnation of vision are ongoing mandates.
8. Criticism of leaders by congregations is a pervasive and painful thorn in the flesh.
9. Leaders can and should quarantine destructive criticism.

10. There is a strong correlation between effective, courageous ministry and a long-term match of pastor and congregation.
11. Long tenure is a joint project between pastor and people.
12. Succession planning will be critical.
13. There is a horizontal revolution happening!
14. Learning communities keep leadership dialogical, energizing, and accountable.
15. These communities are a source of energy, strength, and joy to those in them.
16. Pastors in growing ministries understand and practice appropriate "span of care."
17. The way beyond hoarding ministry is to measure outcomes of transformation.
18. Courageous leaders create congregational cultures where change is assumed, transition is welcomed, and leaning into the future is the default posture.
19. There are strong cases to be made for both evolutionary and revolutionary strategies for spurring change and transition in congregations.
20. There can be great blessings in spiraling complexity.
21. Leadership amidst complexity requires humble, patient sharing.

Don't be fooled by the twenty-one items on this list. These are no "twenty-one immutable laws of leadership." Instead, they represent dynamic, pliable, nuanced, and hard-won lessons from talking with effective practitioners of courageous church ministry. This is an impressionistic portrait of courageous church leadership.

## Conclusion: The Conversations Continue

### A Guitar

When I left home for my freshman year at the University of North Carolina, I was smitten by the urge to learn to play the electric guitar. A childhood of learning classical piano had its benefits but failed to excite in teenage years. God-given perfect pitch helped me figure out that the microwave oven was buzzing in B-flat but gave me precious little help on a fret board. I knew what I loved—hard rock music—but had no clue how to play it. How should I learn?

I began the way many begin: with a Mel Bay chord book and a combination of yard sale and borrowed guitars. Studiously poring over diagrams, I attempted to build finger strength and muscle memory with a few simple chords. I subscribed to *Guitar Player* magazine and began to read tip-filled interviews with great rock guitarists.

Once I learned my way around enough chords to avoid total embarrassment around friends, I began to practice with fellow guitarists, nearly all of whom were far more advanced than me. I was usually quite intimidated, but nearly always found them to be humble, encouraging, and eager to show me tricks. We would "jam," alternating rhythm and lead roles in twelve-bar blues. I knew about three "licks," which I would quickly exhaust before reverting back to the safety of rhythm playing. These sessions were often the occasion for laughable expressions of my inexperience and incompetence, but also the forum for my most accelerated learning.

It was only at this point that I began to take formal lessons from an accomplished local blues-rock guitarist. The lessons would consist of practicing diagrammed scales, such as the staple diatonic scale, until they became second nature. Then, after a short time of jamming, my teacher gave me an old *Bluesbreaker* tape, which featured short instrumental guitar pieces by Jimmy Page, Eric Clapton, and Jeff Beck. My instructions were to play the guitar along with one of the songs until I could mimic the lead note-by-note.

I nearly wore out my cassette player rewinding and forwarding the tape on those songs. But I did learn those short songs. More importantly, I gained a method for learning to play many other songs long after formal lessons ceased. I learned riffs that made me what I am today: a slightly less embarrassing guitar player!

### A Preacher

Princeton Theological Seminary appealed to me as I prepared for the pastorate because it had separate and excellent departments of preaching and speech. While taking technical courses in speech, I was fortunate to receive guidance in an independent study with Professor William Beeners. He gave to me a list of about twenty of the finest preachers in the United States, pointed me to the cassette library, told me to listen to these preachers and write up what I learned.

It was there that I found the preaching of Fred Craddock. While I had used and benefited from his excellent textbook, *Preaching,* in an introductory course, I was electrified when I heard him on tape. This was the finest preaching I had ever heard!

I became a "Craddock junkie." First, I read every book he published. Next, I went to the Princeton Seminary cassette library and listened to every Craddock lecture and tape I could find, taking extensive notes as I listened. Then, I began to search for and purchase tapes of his sermons from other sources, including Candler School of Theology at Emory University, where he was teaching. Finally, I began to take advantage of every opportunity to attend lectures, worship services, and continuing education events where he was speaking.

However, it was two years later that my greatest period of learning from Craddock began. I began to take my favorite tapes of his sermons and transcribe them word-for-word. As I laboriously stroked from cassette to computer, I learned (inductively!) many things about Craddock's style that were never written in his books or spoken in his messages. For instance: that many of his sentences began with a conjunction; that his sentences were very short and with uncomplicated structure; and that his paragraphs rarely exceeded three sentences. In short, I learned elemental aspects of a style of preaching for the ear that impacted my own preaching. It was as if I had learned a Jimmy Page guitar lick or pattern that I could now incorporate into my own style when jamming.

### A Practitioner

But pastoral ministry is so much more than preaching! While I figured out a way of learning how to grow in preaching, leadership was a different matter. As with learning to play guitar and absorbing Craddock, I attempted to cope with the demands of leading a rapidly growing and changing congregation through reading widely, attending events, and continuing education via seminars and a degree program. These attempts to learn and grow were necessary but not sufficient, invaluable but not transformative.

Breakthrough help came when, after much prayer for guidance, I reached out to a pastor whom I had never met. Darrell Boggs was the pastor of Gayton Baptist in Richmond, Virginia, a church about an hour east of where I lived. I don't even remember who recommended Darrell to me, but I was told that his church was "a step ahead" of where the church I led was.

I contacted him and offered to drive to his church, meet him, and take him to lunch so that I could "pick his brain." Doing so, I found that his church had, indeed, worked through some of the issues our congregation currently faced. Darrell was too humble to fulfill my request for him to be my mentor, but offered to "continue the conversations" for as long as I was interested. Eventually, I brought leadership teams from our church to meet with him as well. Upon reflection in years to come, I began to believe that these dialogues were instrumental in our congregation moving beyond the barrier at which we were stuck.

### A Habit

Beginning in the summer of 2000, while working with the Virginia Baptist Mission Board, I began to make it a habit to get to know some of the churches in the nation that most impressed me. If traveling in the area of such a church, I arranged an appointment with the pastor. Most were more than willing to meet with me, tell their story and talk about Kingdom leadership. In the rare instance a personal appointment was not possible, these pastors scheduled a telephone appointment. I gained permission to record these conversations for my own learning, as well as a blessing to share with interested fellow learners.

I applied to these experiences what I learned from absorbing Fred Craddock lessons. I began to transcribe the conversations, and I was always taken aback at the richness of leadership teaching within them. I learned on one level from hearing; on another level from transcribing note-for-note; on yet another level still from juxtaposing one conversation alongside of another. To recall the Erwin McManus image, I find the interviews to be as pieces of a kaleidoscope, which create interesting, ever-changing, and beautiful patterns as they move alongside of one another in different configurations.

### Do It Yourself, with Others

So there is my magic formula. Perhaps it won't take you (as it did me) twenty-five years to figure out how to mine the richness of wisdom around you. Please learn on my dime!

In clinical pastoral education, students learn to do case studies, recounting in written form sketches of conversations with hospital patients. These written case studies then become the forum for group conversation, peer coaching, and personal learning.

One hope I have for this book is that these practitioner conversations will jump-start a set of your own leadership conversations, serving as case studies for you to digest and discuss. But that is only a springboard for a deeper hope: that you will learn to identify the practitioners around you who would inspire you to more courageous leadership. Whether local, famous, neither, or both, my hope is that you will have seen here a model for connecting with and learning from courageous leaders. I suspect you will be surprised at how accessible and eager most are to share what they have learned. For the price of an appointment and maybe coffee or lunch, you can place the most pertinent and pressing issues on the table. As you transcribe, you learn again–from them and about yourself. As you discuss, you may be stimulated to new levels of thought or action. As you collect, you will learn not only from direct interaction with practitioners but, by viewing different practitioners side-by-side, it can be as if practitioners converse with each other. "Is it Brian McLaren's philosophy of radical change or Leith Anderson's incremental change? What is wisest in my situation?"

This would lead to my deepest hope: that conversations about courageous church leadership would multiply exponentially. What we must do in the Kingdom, we must do together, in community. I pray that these conversations will lead to courageous action; that action will lead to transformation of our cultures; and that transformation of our cultures will lead to "on earth as it is heaven" (Mt. 6:10). Amen.

## Christ-Centered Coaching
### 7 Benefits for Ministry Leaders
#### BY JANE CRESWELL

"Coach Jane Creswell is the consummate leader in bringing coaching principles to life in a church or organization. Her words of wisdom will impact your organization more than you can imagine."

■ Laurie Beth Jones, author of *Jesus, CEO; The Path;* and *Jesus, Life Coach*

978-08272-04997

## Recreating the Church
### Leadership for the Postmodern Age
#### BY RICHARD L. HAMM

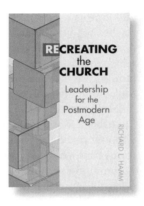

"Dick Hamm asks an essential—and deeply faithful—question of the church: Where are we going? Then, through analysis and insight into both past and future, and with an unwavering commitment to the mission of the church, Hamm points us in the right directions."

■ Wesley Granberg-Michaelson, General Secretary, Reformed Church in America

978-08272-32532

## Pursuing the Full Kingdom Potential of Your Congregation
#### BY GEORGE W. BULLARD JR.

"If you want your church to mature and get beyond the preservation stage and to fulfill God's will for Kingdom growth, then study, read, and pray through this book."

■ Denton Lotz, General Secretary, Baptist World Alliance

978-08272-29846